A Breath Behind Time

Healing by the Goddess and the Revealer

Terri Hector

A Breath Behind Time
Healing by the Goddess and the Revealer

©1999 Terri Hector

ISBN 186163 0700

Cover design by Paul Mason based on a design concept by Terri Jane Winstanley
Internal illustrations by John Harman

Published by:

Capall Bann Publishing
Freshfields
Chieveley
Berks
RG20 8TF

A Breath Behind Time

"A woman's spiritual journey through and within herself to find the meaning of life itself. Using the illustration of mythology, the essence of the internal goddess, she draws the reader ever on through this journey to the surprising conclusion.

Written on several layers in a poetic style, this personal revelation can appeal to a wide readership. Its purpose and aim is to take the reader behind the intellectual maze, to reach deep within their own psyche, to unify and hold in balance the opposing elements of creation that comprise each and every one of us."

Avril B Corke   Amora International

"...intriguingly excellent work.."

The College of Psychic Studies

"I found that Terri has had some extraordinary personal experiences in her life which she is anle to share with us in her book. I am sure other readers will gain something from this book, as I have."

Terry Walters, author of the bestseller *"Who On Earth Am I?"*, published by Amora

Acknowledgements

This book is dedicated to my family and to all those who know that love is the only way forward in order to preserve the Earth. It is with deep felt gratitude, that I give thanks to those people who have given many long hours of their time helping me to complete this book.

Contents

Introduction

Breathing life into the new dawn
The Creators breath melted the dew
For loves offspring, joyous awakening
The earth's spirit entering them anew

I was compelled to write this book with three main threads interwoven to give the reader an insight into the sacred worlds of the spirit. To separate these threads would be like separating the sun, moon, and stars. Each thread relies on the other to strengthen entry into the spirit of love.

Every time I asked the spirit a question about truth or love, the spirit would respond by showing me a vision. The stillness of these visions contained the power to transmit the truth on to my mind, freed of beliefs, opinion, or any other notion trapping me in time. This book was conceived through that truth, teaching me the difference between human and divine love, propelling me beyond the laws of man.

The Goddess She

The first thread is the Goddess *She*, being the pure link to creation in every woman. *She* is my natural rhythm in the universe and link with all Life. *She* will mirror divinity instinctively known by all women, leading you into an unforgettable journey though the inner sacred worlds. Inseparably interwoven is the Godly male guidance of the *Revealer* with his wisdom and unrelenting love, propelling me into the spirit of divine love; safeguarding the balance between the inner spiritual and outer physical worlds; securing my permanent link to the Goddess energy. This

1

guidance can be drawn into all minds if we allow it, but we have been taught to fear it. We have been denied this Divine power through corrupted practices. Nothing can thwart its progress as it finds its expression directly through the people to express its power. We must prepare ourselves with this inner wisdom.

The Flames

The second thread is the *Flames* of initiation, purification and union, interfacing each level of the spirit realms making entry for the initiate as painless as possible. Are you ready to be an initiate?

The spirit of love was compacted into my body in the form of these flames, the essence of all physical life behind time in the spiritual realms. They hold the DNA for the universe. When ignited in the body, either by right lovemaking or by conscious life experience, their fascination holds your attention drawing you nearer to your partner and God for divine union.

The Golden Body

The third thread is the *Golden Body* of love. This is your pure sun or cosmic body, which is now bordering our world to join you to the golden cord, to secure your entry with your eternal spirit into the Paradise Earth. Preparing you for the Golden Age with your beloved with no break in that consciousness at physical death.

This book is inspired by my living experience and heavily condensed with spiritual vision as I was directed to write. I trust this will help to make the crossing easier for the reader. Each myth has been written as a complete story and can be read as such, bringing many areas of interest for the avid spiritual reader. The thread that is most meaningful to you is the truth of where you are.

2

My first conscious entry into the spirit was through the burning cross of purification. Through terror of the mind my spirit twin fled through the Ring of Fire at the centre of the cross leaving me for the safety of the inner spiritual realms; and in my pursuit of Love I followed her.

On my spiritual journey I was introduced to the cowled forms, keepers of the flames, they were my guides as each flame was ignited in my Womb. Contained within the Womb is the creation of all life from the Love that has been made between all men and women of Love, including my husband and myself. And so I came to realise that within my body is the presence of pure Love, the earth Womb. Giving birth to creation at all times. Love draws all life, the materialisation of the creation, through our bodies when we are in a state of Love. With the cleansing and purifying of the world out of the body, all life consciousness flows within.

There are many ways to express Love on this planet, but the most remarkable I experienced was Love beyond death. As my body went into the death energy I heard the compass-ionate cry of the death Goddess calling to take me through the life to-death to- life cycle consciously, keeping me one step ahead of the death energy. The Love of the Revealer maintained my body whilst I went through. At the moment of death He heralded in from the inner spiritual realms the return of my spirit twin, united with the Goddess energy, to work through my body. And it is a miracle that after several near medical deaths whilst being kept alive by the spirit, I was able to maintain the perfection of Love with my spirit-opposite in time. Then I entered into passion through death to join with God through the opposite eternal principal, which for me woman is man, which we all seek in life, but are unable to secure.

While I was dying into and becoming Mother earth I was shown how to embrace and embody Love, the twin spirit. This union purified the body after entering the life to - death to - life cycle taking my place in the natural rhythms of life. I encountered many wonders along the way, guided by my spirit wolf, materialising and dematerialising in the sensory world. I saw them reflected on the inside through the energies of nature moving through my body, including the first birth in the spiritual animal Womb.

After receiving cosmic healing on a UFO, I was taken to see our new life forms preserved and nurtured in the spacecraft. These are our future bodies in our next life. The true resurrection of the spirits, into the body of our race, from the Happy Hunting Ground and the Dreamtime. Along the way my encounter with a spiritual master projected me in to the Golden Age to live with the golden bodies within the paradise earth.

I was shown the devastating truth of reincarnation. We only have this present body in this creation to work through, in the moment, to stop our children suffering karmic fate. The empty physical body reflected from the earth womb into time that knows insufficient Love is a target for false entities of past emotion to fill, when in reality it endlessly waits to be filled by divine Love. We are up against our greatest struggle in human history between the mind and spirit, heading towards destruction as the door to time closes. We must keep spiritually conscious all the way and hold to the greater universal truth of the whole.

I realised that the human race yearns and grieves for this spiritual union of Love yet we cannot consciously die into it, relieving suffering for a painless death, because Love has been distorted out of all recognition. In place of Love, the self and the will have become the ethos of human endeavour in the world, struggling relentlessly to survive, supplanting all Love, creating all suffering. As the barrier of our selfish mind gains momentum and strength through unconscious worldly experience, we can no longer be carried into conscious death to the sacred land through the spirit of Love; nor can we be joined with our beloved opposite on the wings of Love.

I am a witness to the synchronicity of Love, universal impersonal intelligence working to right the people and the planet of all suffering, drawing them ever nearer to their Love to which they are already joined through their divine opposite behind time. In the sacred spiritual worlds beyond death. Only through acknowledgement of their Love for each other can the cosmic porthole open allowing the universal knowledge to flood through their bodies from the cosmos and into their minds. Love is empowerment.

The essence of this story is my holding the balance between the inner and outer worlds; the profundity of it is holding the Love that poured into my body from the cosmos plunging me into the depths of the divine worlds. The power of spiritual Love showed me, in vision, myth and poem, the knowledge of what was taking place beyond time and in my body. This was breathtaking as my divine opposite showed me the beauty of the earthly and spiritual creation and carried me through the cosmic gateway of Love, and into the Paradise earth, the Golden Age.

As a spiritual teacher my aim therefore is to assist people who feel they are trapped in time through the veil between worlds into spiritual life, through conscious death into the life cycle. With love, harmony and divine union, this prepares them for the golden age ensuring the continuation of the creation and their golden consciousness for our New World in the paradise earth.

Prologue

One warm June evening nearing midnight I was talking to a friend who had come to stay on holiday. We were alone in the lounge as the rest of the family had retired to bed. The patio doors were wide open and the sound of the night creatures clearly audible. My friend and I were very different in character but I seemed to be spending more time with her than anticipated while she travelled back and forth between England and the continent.

She did not usually talk much, but this evening she was unusually communicative. She had been having problems of a psychic nature and was asking for help. But before I could say anything her defences went up. Then I felt heaviness in the air and the hairs stood up on the back of my neck. Rising up in front of me I saw a terrifying sight, an invading entity rearing up about to attack me. Gripped by fear and dizziness, I wanted to run but I had lost the use of my limbs. Then suddenly I felt my body shatter like a mirror dropping onto a concrete floor and the room around me began to fade.

Her consciousness swooped down from the sky in the darkness, down to where she could see a long way off an immense fiery burning cross lying in the middle a large field. In terror of the entity she walked quickly through the long wet grass, drawn towards it she instinctively knew it was a haven of safety. At the centre of the cross where the arms met the shaft, was a circle of flames. She fled up the long shaft into the circle of fire with the flames leaping around her, neither hot nor cold. Raising her arms in the air she began to spin and was propelled down through the centre, down through the circle of fire.

My awareness came back into the room, I had no idea where I had been and I was trembling all over. I turned to see the entity still coming after me and I stumbled upstairs in terror and staggered to the bedroom door somehow managing to turn the door handle and collapsed inside on the floor. The entity was after my spirit in its vain attempt to link with God. But driven out by the shock of seeing the entity, my spiritual twin had already gone to the place of safety in the circle of fire.

With this experience I embarked on a quest to unravel the mystery of God and Love and to search for my spirit twin, my link to the Love of God that was lost to me. I was to enter the Ring of Fire many times over the years and wait there at the crossover point in the hope of being re-united with my twin before finally being freed. I had to die consciously; to die into God and Love enabling me to enter the spiritual realms she walked, and to purify myself sufficiently to draw her back into my body and mind. In place of my spirit twin, The Revealer, the Love of man within me came forward to keep my body alive and to guide me on the journey, revealing the path of truth. I was called by the compassionate cry of the Death Goddess to take me through death consciously,(my rite to passage,) and on the path my twin spirit was united with the Goddess of creation.

As time went by the spirit entered my entire mind and this is just a fraction of my journey, the whole being too vast to commit to print. The fiery cross represents conscious death and purification through life experience, the cleansing of the karmic cycle before union with God. Reading this will give the reader a new way into the spirit through the passageway that was opened in my psyche and can be opened up in yours. Not through the shock of the mental fear or hatred I experienced, but through a mind that will enter gradually and peacefully into a world of Love and spirit and finally into the Paradise Earth, the Golden Age.

Chapter 1

The Goddess Answers the Call

In seeking to help others reach that world of love behind the psychic world, I embarked on a journey into the inner spiritual realms. The fascination of it captured my attention, but owing to my frightening experience I was wary to venture in.

The psychic world is fraught with problems. I was alerted to many obstacles as I entered. Sometimes it felt like I was running the gauntlet, but I was pleasantly surprised when I saw I was being shown a way through. I had gone to this place of beauty beyond death when my life had been threatened. Now I had entered the Ring of Fire again, only this time it was for a specific purpose and I knew where I was going.

The Ring of Fire is the pure entry into the earth womb accessed only through love. It is a protected area far beyond the troublesome subconscious mind. All life flows out of it into the physical world and its beauty is astounding.

After working in there for six months I was given a couple of ways to enter without getting tangled in the minefield of emotional problems that would thwart any progress. I had been shown how to bypass the mind with some stunning affects. Suffering did not figure in this teaching.

Reaching this place of love was my daily renewal and problems were purified each day through putting them in the hands a higher power. This was what I was seeking. I had found it, the place I was taken to when I was only three years old where I was introduced to the inner world of light. It was the place I saw my mother enter at the time of her death. Every thing was bright with such blazing intensity and as my little hand was being held by one of these higher beings, I walked in to a world of breathtaking wonderment. I would stand there for what seemed like hours, waking in the morning with peace in my heart with the receding vision.

The Earth Womb was that place of mystery, a great fiery core of unformed life in the centre of the earth where the Goddess resides in her protected glory. As She leads you into the story, it is with this knowledge of the Goddess body in every woman on which I focus most attention.

She lay asleep on the forest floor upon a bed of leaves, which blew, gently around her soft body, yielding to the earth. The animals around her tended to her every need. Awaiting her command they knew instinctively how She felt. But although the animals were safe, there was unease and restlessness, urgency within them and as the pure feeling flowed into Her body through the earth, the Goddess stirred.

She felt the gentle nudge of a wolf at her shoulder and as She turned, the spiritual blaze in his eyes communicated to Her with urgency the crisis that could no longer be ignored. She put Her ear to the ground listening for some sign of a solution but She could feel in the surrounding vibrations that the problem was too big to deal with from where She was.

She was drawn to the dark liquid pool nearby with the moon shining on its surface, silent and still. The dark pool that links to other worlds through the liquid that flows through oceans and rivers, sap and blood, its vibrating substance connecting them all in pure feeling informing them of all creation, if they could only listen to the pulse and birth of all life within it.

She slipped silently from the sacred spiritual world into the dark pool, moving with grace and ease. The moonlight formed a clear passage through the dark tunnel out into the other world, to enter the creational flow of our world with great speed, through the oceans and rivers, into the sap and the blood. She could see the trees were stunted and deformed and as She moved through them all She became conscious that the pure feeling flow of all life had been polluted almost to the point of destruction. The same pollutant had infected the people of the earth and had reached their minds and reproductive systems. They were in a critical state; their creational energy flow was breaking down at an alarming rate. She understood the urgency. Something had to be done.

She cried the call of the Goddess and a wave of beautiful feeling energy sounded throughout the whole of nature resonating with every point of consciousness. Flowers, trees, grass, sunlight, animals, water, all awaited Her command.

Then the Goddess was called again to enter the mind and body of a human being. She followed them through the tunnel of death; out of the mists came the black cowled forms of the spirit world, black flames of Love burning in their eyes. The Goddess saw before Her the body of a dying woman lying on a bed. This was one She could transform. A body containing enough Love for Her to enter it consciously. The cowled forms encircled the bed to keep the balance and maintain the energy as the Goddess cloaked Herself in the elements of time and at Her command with an intense synthesis of energy, a flashpoint, entered into the body of the woman, into a physical body in our world.

*Looking more closely the Goddess realised the body was
similarly polluted and dying into Love of the earth. And that
for Her to work with it, the body's lifeflow of energy must be
contained before it was lost. She began the healing process of
regeneration, igniting the aqua flame within to bring about the
formation of a new body.*

*Through the pool of Love She linked with the woman's mind,
transmitting visions to the woman of another world, the world
of death which is also the world of Love. This was to keep the
woman's mind conscious as she passed through death whilst
maintaining life in the physical body. Then the Goddess
commanded universal Love to enter the body and eliminate all
the dead matter within, and the death energy was purified and
contained in the black flame.*

*High in the heavens had appeared a vortex of gathering
energy. The atmosphere was warm and humid and lightening
flashed and cracked, rolling across the sky gathering speed. A
bolt of light connected to the vortex and was drawn down the
centre into the vortex eye. Diving down towards the woman at
lightning speed it entered her body bringing with it the
purifying qualities of oxygen. It purged the body, sucking into
its own vacuum all the offending poisons contained within the
body and then departed back to the heavens.*

*The world of death and pure Love was thus brought
psychologically and cosmically into the physical world through
this woman's body. Rising from the death bed she was
embraced by the cowled forms and linking hands they danced
together in the dance of death and life in joyous celebration for
overcoming death and bringing of Love, the Goddess, into the
world.*

*With the body thus prepared, looking out from the woman's
eyes, the Goddess sought other women who would help in Her
endeavour to bring more Love onto the earth and to bring them*

close together in Love. For all Love purifies the earth and the sick on this planet.

These visions represent the psychological and cosmic entry of the Goddess into the body. The earth woman's body is now the crossing point between life and death. Enough Love had been stored within it for the Goddess to enter and work in the physical world. And the Goddess creation on earth is looked after by these and other women and men of Love who are joined with her in the spiritual realms (behind time) through the pure feeling body. She lets it stay in their care and keeping.

14

Chapter ii

The Valley of Dried Bones

The Goddess was showing me the beauty of the earth and of all creation. She would show me how to move within the creation to view the natural world, keeping me in touch with any new developments. She would show me how new growth comes into life, giving me the memory code to sing and chant, keeping the cycle of the natural kingdom alive each day as she took over my mind and body. In the background there always seemed to be a more powerful, but gentle, spiritual being watching over her as she made herself known to me.

This being was coming forward in a white haze and as the haze cleared I could see the splendour of him on horseback. The horse was silvery white and he had a golden plume on his forehead that he had carried from the Earth Womb in a blaze of glory: his authority as protector of the purity of woman. This was the Goddess's protector and consort; his only armour was the light he carried, and a staff of crystal as the memory of every thing she represents. Silhouetted by the sun his superiority was very evident. As he rode towards me I was to meet my protector as he beckoned me to cross the sea.

She felt herself being driven down a vortex to a sacred area within her body onto a sandy beach, with the sea gently lapping at her feet. The sea was blood red and she waited there, with the wind whipping around her, knowing she needed to cross. She waded in to swim but the power of the waves pulled her back to the shore. The wind whipped around her stronger now and she thought it would lift her off her feet. It was the vortex leading her back to the shore for a purpose.

She could see now before her a valley filled with dried bones and she understood she could not make her spiritual journey across the sea without a body of energy to keep her linked to the physical world. She walked among the bones in search of a skeleton that was energised. Many crumbled in her path, some had decayed to dust. Looking around she could see a distant glow and instinctively, she knew it was the form she was seeking, a skeleton energised before its physical death. She lay down beside it and the energies of its spiritual body crossed with her own. Her return back into the physical world thus secured, she could now return to the sea and seek again the crossing.

From the shore she could see figures coming towards her on horseback. The horses shone in the light, dazzling, and the riders wore long white cloaks and each carried a staff. The sea was calm. The riders came closer, and she stood there waiting. Then they took formation around her and facing the calm sea, they pointed their staffs towards it. The vortex whipped towards the sea and like an opposing magnetic force, parted the water with its energy, creating a path across the seabed. The riders rode down it forming a column on both sides, their staffs extended towards the centre to enable her to walk through. She followed them through the walls of sea until they had made the crossing to reach the opposite shore. Behind them the waves flowed back, and all that was there was sea.

Then the riders picked her up, laid her across their outstretched staffs and carried her across a desert towards the hot sun and lowered her gently to the ground. There was a lone rider in the distance and she walked towards Him and He offered His hand to her. He said He was the Revealer of all things and that He would show her the energies of the universe. He lifted her up behind Him, and together they rode into the blazing sun. She felt immediately the powerful energies all around her as the rider offered her up to the vortex and it drew her in.

She was gently lifted up the vortex by a myriad of angels circling effortlessly around her. A great river poured forth from the top where she was placed on the back of a patiently waiting, pure white swan. The swan glided down the river and into a vast void, a welcoming black velvety darkness, a place of timelessness and peace. Passing through it to the other side she could see before her a beautiful waterfall and behind it shining a light. She instinctively knew that here was life. As the swan swam nearer, the waterfall changed to a magnificent translucent gossamer veil. It parted for her to go through and she was met by cowled forms robed in white with fire blazing in their eyes.

Coming out of the vision I felt a bright sun burning in my head and the heat in my chest was unbearable. But I knew I had reached something I had been trying to reach for several years. The sea of blood is the emotion that stops you entering the sacred space of the divine. I had sufficiently purified my emotion through Love as represented by the parting of the seas. The door to my psyche into the inner spiritual realms had been opened. The relief was overwhelming and I cried a little. As represented by these myths, this was the entry into my body of the female Goddess energy, reawakened by the critical circumstances in the world. The entry of my male opposite, the Revealer occurred in me when I was a young child. He came into my mind bringing me the peace and protection I needed, and He became a familiar figure to me, standing over my bed at night. In my teens He was with me in the form of a flame, that would flicker before me when I was still. And His presence grew in me until I could take responsibility for the pure male energy, dying into it and allowing it to come into my mind to teach me the truths of the universe.

Chapter iii

The Starry Universe

I had many intuitive realisations in my younger years and somehow, I knew that these were of a far greater intelligence than I. As a spiritual teacher, I was to see many miracles happen in my life. My daughter calling me back to life. My escape from an explosion that wrecked the place where I worked and not least the healing of people when the time was right. I used up all my nine lives, and I know without a doubt that the spiritual intervention in my life saved me all these times.

Pregnant with my second child whilst accompanying my husband on a tour of Germany with the British Forces. I awoke disturbed one morning from what I would describe as a vivid dream of blood running in water. A few days later I woke abruptly and this time the premonition was much stronger. The picture in front of me was of a large vase by a hospital bed, which had been knocked over and instead of water, blood was pouring out. I felt an urgency, which would not leave me, and the realisation that this could mean my life force energy was pouring out of my body. This was accompanied by a very deep feeling of love from my unborn baby, which I could feel intermittently.

Frightened, I explained the premonition to my husband and against the wishes of my friends and family he agreed to let me go home to England to have the baby where I knew I would be safe, and he was to join me later. I was too far into the pregnancy to fly, so I made arrangements to go with a friend by car. Arriving at my in-laws house was a relief as the

18

journey had been a long one. A couple of weeks into my stay, the feeling of love from my baby became stronger and was to serve me in saving my life shortly after the birth and to teach me the real meaning of Spiritual Love.

The Birth

I awoke with a searing pain. On arrival at hospital I was examined and told I was in the second stage of labour. In the next half-hour my beautiful daughter was born, but all was not well with me. I had gone into severe shock and started to haemorrhage very badly.

I could feel the concern of the staff as they tried in vain to stop the bleeding for the blood transfusion was not keeping up with the rate of blood loss. I was feeling weaker by the minute and could only just hear the doctor giving urgent instructions to the nurses around me. He knew that I was already on my way through the tunnel of death and I heard him say, "She's going, put the baby on her quickly and hold it there".

A light drew me through the tunnel and out the other side into an acute awareness, a heightened consciousness. I could see everything. Two nurses were holding my tummy trying to stop the bleeding while the doctor pumped more blood into my legs. Then the hospital room began to move away and nothing mattered.

She was at peace out there in the universe with all the stars, soaring like a bird, enjoying the wonderful consciousness. All life was becoming one and the earth looked magnificent. Then she felt a powerful feeling of Love and compassion rise up in her spirit body, permeating her consciousness. It was instinctively drawing her back to earth, down through the stars, back into the room where her body lay.

I hovered at ceiling level watching all the activity going on around my hospital bed. I seemed to be suspended there, unable to reach my body and after a time, I have no idea how long, a great peace began to descend over me.

She was drawn back into the universe. But then again she felt the massive surge of Love drawing her back to earth. It was her baby calling to her to come back; the same feeling she had felt before the birth, and she could not leave it. Her consciousness took over, pure action, Love for another. In an instant she plunged back into her body and slipped into unconsciousness. Her Love for her daughter meant more than becoming one with the universe in death.

The Platinum Flame

I regained consciousness two days later and for the next few days I was in a twilight world slipping in and out of consciousness. During those days of stillness I could see something bright catching my attention, flickering in front of me, making me follow it until I fixed my attention on to it.

She could see a glow around what looked like a platinum coloured candle flame. It expanded to reveal white cloaked figures with the same flame in their eyes coming towards her and she realised she was being healed.

A Permanent Connection

Although I did not realise it until much later, I had connected permanently with the spiritual flame linking me eternally to the spiritual world. With this I was to be given a complete understanding of the spiritual law of life, through internal telepathy and through vision. With my experience of the power of Love came a deep yearning for permanent union with the Love, and my life experience became the means of learning how to achieve it.

Through the shock of childbirth and the ensuing spiritual experiences, my mind had been swept clean, emptied, leaving a void. The void had to be filled with love to prevent the emotion or psychic forces of the mind flooding back in, and I was to be shown how to do this. To manifest the combustive, purifying energy of love in the body, all opposites have to be brought together. This I did by loving and giving in the simplest of ways starting with my family and loved ones around me.

This is where we all must start, and there is no point in pouring out your Love into the world unless you have first contained it within yourself and passed it in love to your partner. If you love each other, your partner is the person who can most help you realise the beautiful love of the spirit. No spiritual energy can come into the world without a foundation of love to flood into. Your love for each other can help you realise the love of the spirit. I was to find out that love means much more than can be realised with the mind.

The energy of love that we make in the feeling body opens the doorway into the spiritual body. To create this combustive energy of spiritual love is our sole purpose for living. The love dissolves psychological and emotional pain painlessly and radiates out to bond us with the greater universe, the whole of life is then transformed.

Living the truth of this love and manifesting more and more love serves a profound purpose. For love is the doorway into Paradise, the Golden Age where we can achieve the never-ending magnificent consciousness of eternal love whilst here on this earth. To overcome all suffering and immortalise the love between you and your partner, to complete the cycle through death and back to life while still in a body; to link with paradise so the love flows back into this world for eternal creation. That is life's purpose.

Chapter iv

The Explosion

I was still living with my husband and family in Germany and working as a chef in one of the messes. Passing the guard room one morning, I was searched which was unusual, and on entering the mess I was briefed about an IRA bomb that had been planted on the camp and asked to check all the stores and equipment before my staff arrived. All areas seemed to be normal and the day went without a hitch.

Later in the week, I had some strange feeling of fire and saw it surround me at night. I dismissed these feelings because of the bomb scare. But two days later, I woke early with the strong feeling that I must not take the children to work with me that morning. I asked a friend to take them in later on the bus, as sometimes happened when my husband was away.

It was a bright morning when I arrived at work, and as usual I could see some of the officers riding their horses. Sometimes, they would stop and join me for breakfast. This morning I was on my own, preparing the menu and checking the equipment. I was just about to light all the main boilers, when I heard a rumble behind me and an almighty crack opened up in the ground and a searing heat enveloped my lower body.

A powerful jet of gas against my legs hurled me forward and in what seemed a timeless situation but in reality only seconds, it ripped up the floor and lifted some of the equipment; then with its own power blew itself out. I looked around at the devastation before switching all the mains off and walked into my office. The next thing I knew, I was shaking uncontrollably and some of the men had come in to help.

The engineers that came to repair the damage found a leakage of gas from the main valve underground. The kitchen had large underground gullies, which took most of the explosion, and so I was lucky to get out with only burns to my legs. If I had not listened to my intuition very probably my children would have been badly hurt because where they would often stand was the exact spot where the explosion had taken place.

Chapter v

The Revealer

The greatest purification through Love occurred when I was faced with adversity and the overcoming of pain. Once the suffering was sufficiently purified I was given enough vital energy from the experience to ignite another spiritual flame, to interface the spiritual and physical worlds, unifying the opposites.

Pain Barrier

The morning following a minor operation I was at home recuperating when I experienced a delayed allergic reaction to one of the drugs I had been given during the surgery. The whole of my body was seized with violent muscle spasms. At the local medical centre I was seen immediately by the doctor who examined me, administered a tranquilliser and said he would arrange my transport home and visit me after surgery to see how I was doing. But immediately I began to experience even more severe muscle spasms in my neck and chest and it felt like I was being crushed to death. I started to drift in and out of consciousness and the pain was excruciating.

Suddenly a great authoritative male voice spoke out through me telling the doctor not to send me home and instructing him how to treat me. The astonished doctor examined me asking me how I could speak like this, saying it was unknown medically for the voice to change in this manner. He called for a colleague to examine me and they decided to send me to hospital for the treatment and he was so concerned he stayed with me until the ambulance arrived. I was only partially aware of what was happening for an amazingly beautiful feeling had come over me.

As I descended into unconsciousness I was rushed off to hospital. I could hear the ambulance siren and feel the motion of the vehicle, then all faded from my conscious mind and I became acutely aware of an infinite intelligence looking out of my body. This intelligence, an all-encompassing spiritual power, was keeping my body alive until I reached the hospital.

The Milky Way

She instinctively moved into the point of awareness to connect with the intelligence and found herself speeding deep into the universe, and on towards the milky way. She felt at home and at peace. She saw a sudden brightness of incredible intensity, and for a split second the whole of her being - body, mind and spirit came together and she felt complete. Then her body went limp and a split second later the crushing effect started again.

The intelligence was acting as an all pervasive power throughout her body to override the drugs and spasms. At an indescribable speed she was back again with the stars and the intelligence, moving into the brightness. She was held there for a while in timelessness and from this star an even greater expanse of the universe was revealed. For her, the doorway to the universe had opened.

It was my personal star that I would meet again at death to become it and then pass through it, my porthole to the cosmos.

The antidote to the drug that had caused the allergic reaction brought me out of the trauma and later that day I returned to consciousness muttering about the experience. I could not understand what had happened to me and it was particularly traumatic that no one else could either. Confused and searching for an explanation I was introduced to a psychologist who telephoned me from his clinic. To my relief he understood my experiences and explained they were of a spiritual nature. He could not help me to any great extent, but advised me to pursue a spiritual life. I did not know what this meant but I was aware I needed to make my internal experience conscious externally in my living experience.

The Teacher

Then the Revealer made Himself known to her. Out of the spiritual fire He came and said: "I am the Revealer. To you I will make all things clear". She recognised His voice, she had heard it before at the surgery speaking through her body. He told me He was coming into my mind bringing me spiritual knowledge. I felt a profound sense of Love which induced an incredible stillness throughout my being, allowing the spiritual knowledge to be imprinted on my mind in the form of visions and teachings.

Spiritual Love always shows you what you need to understand in even the most perplexing situation, if you are able to take responsibility for making the negative energy conscious in your life. I was shown everything was as it should be. I only had to look within and link up with my star, the light I was taken to as a child, the doorway to the universe.

The Revealer became my teacher transforming me mentally to bring together the spiritual and physical worlds as one in me. He would make His presence known to me by putting me into a state that was so peaceful I could not move, gently helping me to get to know Him better. He told me at all times to listen for His vibration and He would direct me through spiritual vision, manifesting in a parallel dimension. Pure vision is truth conveyed through Love; it never changes and is absolutely still. Not all people experience vision as I do for each one of us is unique and the energy manifests differently according to the individual.

For many months after these experiences I was in a state of shock and void. The Revealer explained that I had broken almost all my ties with the past, and not to be afraid when at times I felt extremely disorientated and ungrounded. For this is what shock does to a person, radical but very effective. He went on to say that although these ties hold the world together I would learn in time to secure myself with the golden cord of Love.

The Revealer explained I had gone through the pain barrier in my mind. The pain had thrust me over the void, separating me from time, creating enough space for life's natural painkiller to be released in me. Reaching the other side of the void I had secured the pain killing energy, putting my mind and body into deep suspension while healing took place. Most of humanity has forgotten this energy exists and is unable to utilise it in difficult circumstances.

The void is the waiting area to enter into the opposite side of the brain in man and woman to balance the opposites, bringing great relief in all situations because of the supremacy of its equilibrium. Entering the space and keeping it pure for God allows the creational flow to flood its power into the body, enabling the body to be supported by linking you with all life.

The Revealer said this would help me in the future for we must all master or cross over into this area in life or death to be with the opposite. It is the natural expression of what keeps the earth and our bodies alive within the creation. By connecting with the flow of life, the feeling body within linked to nature allows nature the uninterrupted freedom to flow within our body. It aids in healing the body by realigning the cellular structure, keeping the human and animal body alive and healthy with the free flowing action of all life as one whole. It is our natural right to life.

Slowly I began to realise I was seeing the mental and emotional energy that had been ejected from my body through the shock of my experience, coming back to fill the void, to claim its source. The Revealer explained that it is past psychic energy, now the death energy, the false energies of spirits or old memories of the past trying to live in the present by claiming the mind without concern for my welfare. I was shown the power of the present as these past energies were purified by the powerful Love of the Revealer in the moment they entered my mind. I was transported consciously down into the earth Womb to be kept purified; breaking my link with the mind. Then my body could be worked on spiritually without repercussions.

But inevitably I was unable to stay in the earth Womb all the time for I needed to return to the physical world to care for my family and balance the inner experience with the outer manifestation of it. My body had to deal with what remained as dead matter and a couple of days later I was to receive the incredible power of spiritual healing. The more energy entering me and being transformed the more visions I had of the sacred lands within. I had to live this truth through pure action in my life to prevent the emotional and psychic forces flooding back into the mind and body, keeping it pure. The void was a place of infinite mystery and fascination for me during this time.

The wholeness we call our spiritual life encompasses the inner spiritual and outer physical realms, the earth Womb within the body and life's experience with creation out in the physical world. Holding the two in balance is one of our hardest tasks for there is little written on that subject and the thinking mind is not programmed for the expanse of the experience. For it to be achieved all has to be lived through action in the physical not just thought about in the confines of the intellectual imagination of the mind. This balance of opposites is what I have brought about in my body through my living experience.

The Voice of God

I now know that mental psychic energy is the energy that causes everything in the universe to decay through time and impersonally destroys everything in its path. Although it is a decaying energy it also has the purpose of making people still. In trauma or crisis you have to go with the energy, and the more still you are the more power you can gather to bring in the equilibrium, and go into the magnificent realm of the earth Womb and be healed.

But as the mental and emotional energies pressed onto me for integration to be made conscious, it caused me a lot of physical problems. Not yet being able to fully reach my spiritual nature within, my physical body in the outside world was still in chaos. I was in bed for several months, I could not walk and was having physiotherapy every day. Stillness was forced upon me.

The spiritual energy intervened to show me whatever I needed to know to transform the mental psychic energies that pressed on me, to bring them back to their own reality: purity. I realised that my mind and memory was dissolving, undergoing a complete transformation because of the shock I had been through. How long it would take I did not know, but I was about to experience profound healing and soon to realise the power of the spirit.

All through this time the spirit showed me it is only the body in time that suffers. I was raised above the suffering and connected to the beauty of my spiritual being. This freed me from the devastating blow of the shock I had experienced, and I was taken into the beautiful place called the earth Womb to be given knowledge.

Healing

Looking out of the window from that room she saw a blue coloured vortex of energy reaching through the sky and out into the universe. She had no idea what it was but she had the strangest feeling that it was pulling her through it each day. Her awareness was going through the vortex to another galaxy somewhere in the universe. Perhaps linking to the star of brightness again.

Through the Revealer's impersonal Love I became more and more still, moving further and further behind time into the sacred lands. There is only power in stillness when you go behind time and see the movement of time, which has power to bring the spiritual presence into the physical world.

In this most breathtakingly beautiful place I was taught spiritual truth through the consciousness of my being, free of any mind involvement. Universal energy resonated within my body flooding my mind with the stillness that goes hand in hand with consciousness and instantaneous understanding. Of that which always is and that which will always be, after we have been and gone from this earth. Universal truth and consciousness is in everyone if they can reach it with their Love; by looking into the purified mind with no past.

Over the weeks of stillness much was revealed through vision. I was taught about the purified mind symbolised by angelic forms from the angelic world, pure spirit represented by fire. I was taught about pure egoistic awareness, the individuality you retain after physical death. Through vision, without visualisation or imagination, I observed the truth of the universe that is. And by the grace of these teachings I was shown that I am, impersonally, part of everything that is.

The Cowled Presence

One day, as she lay there she saw around her six cowled figures with white consecrated fire in their eyes. A voice spoke from within her being, "Would you like to get up and walk?" "Yes" she replied and the voice told her to turn over but she could not. The voice repeated the command but again she could not, she did not have the strength. Then a beam of intense light shone from their eyes directly into her body, which was lifted and turned over. The rays moved down to her lower spine with a loud buzzing noise and she was turned on her back again.

My legs started to move and I got out of bed and was able to walk after a couple of months of scarcely being able to move. If I felt any pain in my body my consciousness had only to re-enter the earth Womb and it was instantly dissolved. I was shown in several ways that if you detach from the physical mind you can overcome anything in life. I would sink into the Womb and be bathed in its beautiful fires. But, although this helped me greatly, it seemed like an age in the physical body.

I became more and more still over the next few months and I began to realise the message the Revealer was trying to convey. I needed the union of both psychic and spiritual energies to keep my body intact, for it is pure psychic energy that holds the body together, as I was soon to experience. All this happens painlessly within the body if the balance of all opposites is right. My physical body had gone into chaos and to rebalance it my conscious awareness was taken down to the earth Womb so that my body could be worked on psychically and spiritually, to bring about the balance needed for equilibrium. For having experienced this once you can reconnect with it at any time.

Chapter vi

The Descent into the Spirit

The Revealer came to me and said He would show me the mastery of the universe. The way to gather energy and acknowledge universal love.

She had seen them before; white doves coming out of the bright spiritual flame. They would fly around her bringing with them infinite peace. For they are the supreme spirits, the symbol of the truth of all life, from the purified mind. They can transform into many things, they can be what they need to be to teach her in demonstration of universal truths, changing into the cowled forms, the presence of the spirit cloaked so she could see them.

With eyes of silver spiritual fire, the cowled forms led her down a rotating tunnel of shining multi- colours; a marble pathway and they entered into a magnificent place, the divine Womb and Tomb. A crystalline structure of compacted Love through which flows all of life's creation; a magnificent crystal tomb filled with angels singing and a multitude of still and silent spiritual forms; down to where the brightly coloured flames burned, interweaving like flickering folds of glowing velvet. Three cowled spiritual forms glided towards her, each pausing in turn to gather up and offer her a flame: green, cobalt blue and silver. Green - the natural universe; blue - the divine will; silver - the divine spirit that permeates all life within and without. She acknowledged each of them and welcomed the flames into her spiritual body.

The Revealer walked her around the remaining flames in the Womb explaining what they represented. Platinum - the flame of compassion; silver and gold - the sun and moon energy; pink - innocent Love .He said that black and white together- the two sides of spiritual and physical life is one of the most difficult to balance. Pure black - the flame of pure Love and death made conscious; magenta-violet - male and female union before final union with God energy. Crystal - the creational energy of the feeling world, purely for woman preparing her for God; black-red - impure emotion; light-blue - pure animal essence; aqua - physical cell and skeletal regeneration.

He then brought her before an awe inspiring pillar of fire flickering with the cobalt-blue flames of omnipotent power. The compacted energy, the eternal essence of all people who have ever lived, some of whom were standing behind her in their pure spiritual form. Majestically, the Revealer moved into the pillar of flame and she felt a command vibrate through her body to connect with the three flames she had absorbed earlier and to hold them in her body.

She was drawn irresistibly into the blue pillar and as she floated up, her essence was blended with the breathtaking rhythm of the universe that rushes through the pillar like a torrent and the feeling of it was compacted into her body. Then the Revealer led her out of the pillar to join with a host of angels resonating with the same energy, instilling it in her like an inrush of air so that she breathed in unison with the spirit.

Two cowled forms appeared at her side, one her father, the other her mother representing, she recognised, eternal Love. The Revealer gently guided her through the myriad of silent spiritual forms and she could feel their sweetness all around her and emanating from their blazing eyes, acknowledgement of her union with the divine spirit. He told her that she would need to link with all the spiritual flames to support her body in life after death, enabling her to continue her life here on earth

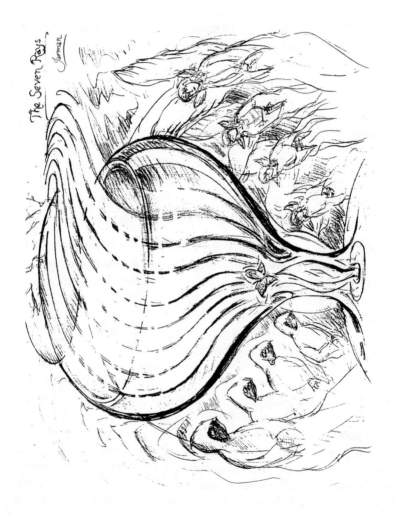

The Seven Rays

by entering the life to-death-to life cycle. And that she would need to prepare herself for the breath of life.

I am looking at the beautiful place where the doves come from. Where the spiritual fires burn, where the alchemy of physical life and of the spirit coalesce, where the transformation of all matter takes place. I know this place as the earth Womb and Tomb, the purpose of which is to give birth to all forms of life and to receive all back when life's journey has ended.

Here all things come together, everything from the physical passes through into the spiritual and then into the eternal realms. Here the chemistry of the universe is encapsulated, where all spiritual records are kept, a DNA code bank for the universe. It is the place of balance and harmony, of oneness and peace, of supreme knowledge, eternal wisdom and stillness. This divine Womb and Tomb of life and death is within every body on this earth.

A Colour Meditation

This meditation is excellent for gathering energy left outside of you, starting the process for renewal. All the flames can be gathered into the energy centres inside of the body each day. It would be good to memorise the colours before you start. It is impossible to take in any more energy than is already yours.

This is a way of self-healing, balance and induction into the earth womb. In our every day life we leave an enormous amount of our life force energy outside of ourselves, particularly our love. This depletion of energy is very detrimental to our well being, we cannot expect to feel spiritual love if we do not keep a good supply of energy within.

The energy of creation doesn't have a problem moving in and out of your body, but it does have a problem with containment.

The ideal is to keep the body free of invading parasites or entities by purification through each flame. Anything can be dealt with inside our being if we know how to contain and purify. Energy ejected outside of us is in effect more harmful, taking into account that on re-entry the energy has been multiplied by the forces gathered on its journey. The time lag can be considerable, dislocating you from the problem. It then takes on a life of its own and becomes a past life.

After making yourself comfortable and putting on your favourite music, if that helps you relax, close your eyes.

This meditation will be more meaningful to you if you can stay as conscious as possible, but if you do fall asleep no matter, you will have achieved something. This meditation is very rejuvenating, helping with stress relief and balancing your body after a hard day's work.

When using colour the mind will relax and gradually switch off, necessary if you want to quickly bypass the emotional field. If you try to go through the mind you can get caught up and disturb the emotions. They are best left alone at this stage. The pure energy outside of you is conscious; in other words, it gives to all people equally. It will certainly serve you if you allow your body to vibrate at the same level. It is all around you in the creation. Begin by assisting the energy back into the body by breathing in the first colour.

Red

Red is the most vibrant. This colour will move down to its place just below the navel. Put your attention down on that part of the body and begin to breathe in through your nostrils, slowly and rhythmically for several minutes or until you feel a little more at peace.

If you see this colour, all the better, it will help relax your mind, but it is not necessary to try to visualise. You must let the intelligence of the energy work for you in its own way. It is much better to try and feel the sensation of it when it's gathering in you. Eventually, any negative energy will be purified as it re-enters the depth of the body through the blood system.

Green

This colour represents the female in nature. It gravitates towards the third eye in a spiral action before entering the body, moving down into the upper part of the body assisted by your deep breathing. It is the colour green in its many shades that relaxes the muscular and nervous system.

Keeping your attention in the centre of the body, breathe in deep breaths, feeling if possible the green spiral around the top part of the head. Penetrating the third eye, the spiral moves speedily into the upper part of the chest beginning to relax you. If you feel yourself sliding into it, let go, you are always looked after with pure energy.

These energies are more intelligent than you could know; they are pure and work for your wellbeing. As you feel them doing their job remember, that nature made your body so it can support and heal you too. The worst that can happen is you feel spaced out, becoming at one with the earth. Let the energy find its own way, it will eventually flood the bottom chambers of the heart.

Gold

Gold is the colour that does most of the work in dealing with past energies. It represents the male in all its splendour; it can cause tremendous heat in the body while healing takes place, it takes care of the past very efficiently. Sometimes the heat will disperse down into the arms and hands.

A microscopic point in the solar centre of the body, this tiny speck of intense golden power, can be activated to enhance your wellbeing. This is the first step in reaching your golden consciousness.

Now continue with the breathing exercise, you will see more of what I am endeavouring to explain as we go through the book, still keeping your attention in the centre of the body. Know that the golden energy is ready to pour in to your body at any moment. It enters the body at the top of the head, assist it in with your breathing. Open your being to the universe, let the higher powers have access to your body.

As you feel this cosmic energy entering and working for you, move into its motion, be at peace. You will know when it has connected to the golden sun point within you, by either heat or expansion. Keep breathing and assisting the golden energy through the top of the head. When you have taken in as much as you comfortably can we will move on.

Cobalt Blue

Blue, as you will read further in the book, is the mastery intrinsic in our physical world, bringing everything into form and removing its essence when all life expires.

In the ethers of this colour you are drawn towards the creator for sacred and divine union.

Keep your breathing as rhythmically even as possible, with your concentration still in your chest yield to the blue vapour. The blue vapour will gravitate towards you entering the body at the bottom of the throat or thyroid area. Concentrate on taking this vapour into the lungs for now. As you continue, the vapour will condense down into a tiny flame and although you cannot see it, it is ready to enter the body. Sometimes you can recognise its presence if you are very sensitive.

When you have filled your lungs for several minutes there will be an over spill. Begin to breath the blue energy down the spine, taking it a little deeper as you progress, until it reaches the coccyx dissolving all unwanted energy in its path. You will feel that many of the unfavourable energies will have shifted after the containment, then been neutralised.

This meditation is one of first ones I teach my students for renewal each day. Once you have mastered this meditation the other energies will draw towards you automatically. Each colour is explained in the different chapters.

There are many more advanced methods, which I teach for balance and well being. It is far better to learn to control your own unfavourable energies than to put them in the hands of others. All these pure energies when compacted back in the body will help you to become much more balanced and spiritually aware.

Chapter vii

The Crystal of Living Matter

Startled, I looked at the clock, it was 3.35am. I was not accustomed to being woken early in the morning. I saw a light radiating in the corner of the room and heard a voice telling me to lie still. It was a commanding voice, but gentle so I felt no fear. The voice spoke from the light, saying, "I am going to show you the mysteries of the universe". I then saw a beam of pink light with a deep blue colour radiating from it rise up from my feet, through my body and stopped at my forehead where its energy penetrated my third eye, and I was transported down into the void, in timeless suspension.

I had no idea where I was going, but I seemed to be encased in its powerful energy field moving smoothly with the colours swirling around my spirit body. I could see an intense point of spinning light an immense distance away and I was irresistibly drawn towards it until I stopped before it, so bright that I was unable to look. But the voice intervened and told me to look in front of me.

The gleaming facets of a spinning crystal caught her eye. As it revolved, prisms of light, beautiful coloured rays beamed out throughout the earth Womb connecting with the spiritual fires. And in each ray were cowled forms floating out from the crystal and down to the flames. Several thousand of them departed from the crystal to go into their designated flame. Fascinated she drew closer.

*In the centre of the crystal something was metamorphosing, a
pulse of energy formed from living matter, a living intelligence
formed to oversee the creational energy to bring about the earth
Womb's new creation. It was moving; prisms of light pulsated
from within the crystal with a blinding intensity unknown in
our world. The pulsating intelligence collected around the
outer edges of the crystal to form three points of scintillating,
powerful energy. One the universal law, the second the sacred
knowledge and the third the movement from the divine into the
physical.*

*The silence and stillness held everything in suspension. Then
the crystal began to implode, and the three energies broke
away to form strategic points of power within the earth Womb.
From the surrounding flames the cowled forms turned in
acknowledgement, and each directed a beam of light back onto
the crystal. She could see renewed life forming at the centre,
bursting open to bring the creational energy into the Womb,
contained within its own energy, the blueprint for a new
universe to come into being.*

*Then the crystal imploded, completely disintegrating and in its
place was created a blue pulsating form. A synergy of two
opposite energies: a pulsating dome and a protective surface
covering. She could sense the intelligence of the pulse in the
centre. It beckoned her forward and she floated towards it.
Passing through the energy field she lost consciousness for a
short time, then found herself floating inside the dome. She
was gently lowered into the energy and her consciousness
engulfed in a blue, azure and soft white haze. Peace enveloped
her spiritual body.*

She heard a voice speak.

*"I am going to show you the secrets of the universe.
Into you I will breathe the breath of life.*

I am going to set you and others like you, free.
Stay with me. Be still."

The voice gently cascaded through the energy field around my spiritual body. The crystal of living matter reflects a transforming energy as it rotates, to keep the matter of the physical body pure and to lift the vibration of the body to prepare it for its next dimension to enter the flames. The spiritual energy from my body was bursting through to my mind unifying and transforming the past psychic (mental) energy that had pressed itself onto me after the shock, the void was being filled.

The Silver Flame

Several cowled figures came around her, covering her with a veil and ushered her up marble steps to the edge of a moat surrounding one of the fires. As she was led through the silver liquid it ran up her legs to her head changing to silver the colour of her spiritual body and the veil she wore. Then moving onwards and into the fire her body was submerged in a cool and soothing effervescence.

Released from the fire she joined the cowled forms encircling the flames. Then she felt something so powerful permeate her body she thought she would lose consciousness. A feeling of great Love emanating from someone close and turning she saw her mother's face. In that instant of recognition, her features were wiped away leaving only a skeletal framework, carrying the silver flame for eyes. Then in an instant she was gone.

The encounter was so powerful my physical body could bear it only for a short while; my first real encounter with impersonal Love. I felt it was worth experiencing above anything else. I knew the feeling was the power of Love because I felt the Love physically in my body. I was at peace and this was in itself a transformation. When the psychic mental and emotional energies merged within my body, they were neutralised by this spiritual energy within and I could feel intense warmth radiate through my body followed by a deep peace almost too exquisite to bear. These contrasting visions were an indication of how rapidly the psychic energy pressing on me was being purified, bringing the mental and spiritual energies together, unified in Love and knowledge.

Seeing my mother helped me to know where I was and the Love she conveyed comforted me. Her maternal Love, the most powerful Love in life before meeting ones partner, was the means for me through my feeling body to build the bridge, to reach the earth Womb again and again.

The cowled forms are the purified ego, the pure feeling of all Love that has taken place on this earth who come to people like myself and others to embrace us. They have made the long struggle over time and space through Love and courage to reach this point in the microcosm. These cowled forms are the keepers of the flame and they are of such a high order that they have no mind or emotion, only action and feeling.

I have seen them come into the physical world in the form of light sources and move into peoples bodies to cleanse and make them whole again before they leave the earth. This healing work helps people to reach their eternal bodies before they leave the earth, so they can become the new race of beings on the new paradise earth.

Balance And Equilibrium
I was thrust into this place of stillness and knowledge many times to be taught and to be healed. Then I would come back into the physical world with renewed energy to carry on living my life doing the things I loved most, looking after my children and trying to function in everyday life. The Revealer was closer to me than my breath at this time, as there was no-

one in life to help me, except those people, in particular my husband, who with their Love gave me the reflection to perceive the wonders of our physical earth.

The Revealer directed me to keep the spiritual and physical worlds, the inner and outer, in balance at all times. For nothing can be achieved in one without the reflection in the opposite. I set about igniting more flames to interface the two worlds on all levels. The flames already burning in my Womb, ignited by the Love of the Revealer, gave me the power to open up new spiritual dimensions and to purify my physical body sufficiently to maintain the equilibrium. I set about clearing the area of my subconscious mind by exposing and facing things, which one normally tries to avoid. Such as not giving in to suffering and emotion and not letting the past dictate the future.

The Place of Mystery

As the spirit of Love in my body became more conscious I developed more vision. I would see angels surrounding me as I descended into the earth Womb that holds within all the archangels and the mastery of the universe. All opposites cosmic, physical and spiritual were joined in me, and I was shown how I could work with people to help them. And so my Love for people grew deeper and deeper.

The Revealer showed me that we are all joined. We can impersonalise Love by dropping our expectations and emotional hold on people, ceasing all wanting from life and ridding ourselves of the barrier to true Love, then we can truly have this beautiful union with life and Love and all people on the earth. And this will truly make the Paradise on earth.

The Womb and Tomb, the world of balance and harmony, is indeed a magnificent place of healing and all people who enter there are transformed. I take each person into the Womb and

Tomb and help them to reunite with their opposites in there to bring them back to Love. Through vision I can explain what they are bringing into the world. It brings about in each person their own unique awakening and also their own unique consciousness as they enter spiritual love. By bringing these two together they can manifest this beauty as a living reality on the earth.

This is the way the Revealer shows me love. So vast is the beauty of the womb it can overwhelm me at times. Those people who are purified enough can see and understand what is being presented here. Everybody who has worked through compassion can see the eternal union of all life. The earth Womb of harmony and balance is far more vast and profound than mere words can convey. It is a place of mystery, where anything can happen in the fires. Stillness and balance are the most profound things that work on a person's life, whether it is to relieve illness or mental torment.

After entry into the earth Womb people's lives become much more balanced. They are then able to do things with a clear mind instead of with a confused mind which, naturally, only leads to more confusion. In the stillness, is the power to manifest the combustive energies of Love in the physical body to bring Love into the world. Once that stillness has been brought about in a person then it can be used to purify and enhance their life.

Chapter viii

The Womb and Tomb, the Cup of Plenty

With life and death all around us, it seems natural to be inquisitive about where we have come from, or were we are going. Why should life and death be so painful? What is it in our character that we cannot make sense of this phenomenon? I must have been asked this question hundreds of times.

Having forgotten our original memory, we can't see that we are just a reflected image in time from the centre of the earth's molten core, like the flowers and the animals! Animals feel pain, but their dying seems to be more natural and less painful then ours. All the energies for purification are random, if we could receive the energies as the animals do we would not suffer so deeply. You only have to look into the natural kingdom to realise this. They are not attached to their pain as we are.

What makes it necessary to go through pain when reaching the higher states of being? I have never met anybody who has reached enlightenment without some form of suffering.

We take on so much distorted past. Purification of that past is one of our biggest heartaches and the least understood. Whether it is loss of a loved one, job, home, an illness or persecution in some form, we overlook this knowledge not always seeing the true facts in life. These are all life situations, which we fail to accept as the cleansing process. Right thinking does have a purpose to play in how you get through a situation, if only to take the old beliefs away. Try telling that to the person who has had some heart rending news. Most people never recover from a major shock, unless they can turn it in to some sort of action or good, to help the healing process begin.

One of the biggest areas in my work is helping people understand that God has not persecuted them and that their thinking did not get them into their state either, causing more suffering for them. No pure energy in the natural world is personal, it is only made personal by the mind, so why do we torment ourselves.

The general thinking in the new age movement is, as you think, so it is reflected in the body. Well, I have met many so-called mental cases with no physical illness and many physically ill people with no mental problems. Why do spiritual people perpetuate suffering? We can't possibly begin to heal in this way.

Under mans law there is no perfect solution to purification. Before the religious mind was instilled in us, all disease was kept in check and eliminated by group healing. The individual was never the main focus of attention. The earth people knew of disease but were alert enough to keep it from entering their bodies. When sections of their society broke away, they failed to follow the laws of the earth renewal for an extended life. This is when the web of life weakened and the outsiders took over.

At the beginning of time earthman and earthwoman were powerless to resist the attraction and temptation of the gods. The earth people were allured with their charismatic ways and in no time at all they had been taken over. This severed them from their true identity and their power to purify and heal. We have been de-empowered from that time by putting our authority into the hands of others.

Why do pregnant women have all the pain in labour, the woman appears to take it all? You would think with all the pressure the child endures in the birth canal that there would be more damage caused to the unborn. But the truth is, the child is still connected to the earth womb by the umbilical cord, where any pain is neutralised by its cleansing powers through the purifying flames. The very place we have disconnected from.

We seem to overlook this simple fact, if the birth is normal, we should be helping the mother to connect to this place too. The reason for stating this fact is that most pain can be removed if we go back to our original place, the womb of all life. This is the earth womb coming alive in me, continuously teaching my mind from within the purpose of all life and the facts of living in our times.

Earth Womb

The earth Womb is where everything from the sacred place of the spirit manifests into the physical world through the goddess womb that is in every woman. I see it as an enormous crystal cavern, holding all the cosmic and earth energies of light cloaked as the cowled forms to make the spiritual presence visible to me. It holds the spiritual fires containing the eternal creation and regeneration of all life, in the form of skeletal bodies ready to generate new life on the planet. It is the earth and physical Womb represented in myth as the Holy Grail containing the still pool of Love and life, the sacred blood and sap. Suspended within and behind time it is ready to flood forward into our new spiritual era here on earth.

The earth Womb is the pulse of the universe where all life waits suspended for the omnipotent presence to strike. The Love is in our being, awaiting its physical manifestation. As with the split of the first atom, the Divine Will alone has the power to bring it into being. At God's command the heavenly bodies of the cosmic male and female principle, the sun and the moon, form the eternal essence. The union of the opposites in reflection, in a synergy of swirling energies, form into a great light that passes down the blue pillar.

The male energy divides into left revolution and the female into right revolution moving out from the pillar in a great circle of light cradling the fires of the compacted universe, encompassing the whole alchemy of the earth Womb.

Here the omnipotent presence holds and cradles the earth Womb, the great cup of plenty, the cup of light holding the sun, the moon and the stars. Until the timeless moment when the consciousness of God focuses into the cup, the great earth Womb gently rocks to create the alchemy for the manifestation of all life. Then the rivers of life begin, gushing forth at the moment of birth. The stem of the cup is the means to channel the river of life and light down to the earth and the base the means to spread it on the earth creating the chalice of plenty. When the sun and the moon move down the central shaft of light into the earth, Mother earth then cries her pangs of birth.

The great eruptions herald in a new creation not to be feared, for Mother earth through woman's Womb on this earth is giving birth at all times. The new creation is to bring the stars into our minds with a wonderful teaching for humankind. The twin suns, one within the solar centre of the body and the other outside in the cosmos, reflect each other with the sun on the outside drawn to the sun within the body; the golden atoms of the male and female cosmic bodies. Together they rotate and reflect to energise each other inside the body to keep matter pure by the love that is made and kept in balance by the powerful magnetic pull of the new moon. Their union at all times ensures that we may move into a new creation as purified cosmic earthlings prepared for the Golden Age.

The Life Thread

Another remarkable aspect of the earth Womb is the "life thread" a myriad of coloured fibre-optic threads of light which lead out from the earth Womb to the physical universe, to each physical body and the whole of the cosmos. These same connecting threads of light draw energy from decayed life in the physical world, through the creational flow of the feeling body, the veins of Mother earth, back to the centre where it is reconstituted through the fires of the earth Womb back into the whole.

The World of Harmony and Balance

The inner world of harmony and balance in the earth Womb and Tomb became a spiritual sanctuary for me. I would descend down the white vortex of energy into the very essence and being of myself. There I would encounter a veil of the most beautiful translucent gossamer I had ever seen. It transmitted light and I could see behind it there was life, though I did not know what kind of life.

As I got nearer, the light would part the veil and I could step inside. Once inside I could see two beautiful people, the kind of people you only know through spiritual feeling; beautiful cowled figures with burning eyes of consecrated white fire. They would escort me through a blaze of light into an even deeper and more profound place, a great hall of such magnificence unknown in the physical world. A very still place, with a stillness of unbelievable mystery but where, I knew, all life was contained within.

Over the many years since, as I continue to look into it, nothing has changed for it is eternal. It can manifest profound truths and here in this wonderful place I was introduced gradually to the many cosmic flames that burn within it.

Building the Bridge

The purpose of the earth Womb and Tomb is to bring unconditional universal Love and knowledge into the world. By entering this world of harmony and balance I have built the bridge that allows access from the physical world back to the transforming and purifying spiritual flames at all times. Entry into each flame came to me with both a spiritual and physical experience. The significance of each flame and entry into its divine presence is revealed in the following pages.

It is my life's work to take people inside the earth Womb within their own bodies and for them to blend with the spirit of truth in the earth Womb.
This reveals itself to everyone of us who is cleansed enough to enter, for the souls of the earth who have suffered enough and have had enough experience of life to know that this is the way home. With the closing of a door in the physical world comes an opening into the great mystery and wonder of the spiritual realm calling you, telling you it is time to go home.

Chapter ix

Divine Will

I had no idea when I started my spiritual work just how it would develop, I certainly never envisaged becoming a spiritual teacher. It redesigned my mind over the years and to see the earth womb take form within me was truly breathtaking.

Speaking with many people over the years I realised life must have its mystery but it is spiritually and physically here and now, not in some heaven somewhere. That is where we go astray, de-empowering ourselves by losing our true earth spirit, which we have embodied from the beginning of time.

Our earth spirit can be brought back into the body through the power of the flames and particularly the blue flame. This energy is our entry into the sacred realms, the perfection that is in all people.

The blue flame of the divine will is compacted universal intelligence that works with me and for me, which it is my privilege to serve. It protects me as I descend down through the subconscious, and takes me into the place of harmony and balance. It is not I the person, but the spirit working through the blue flame that does it all for me. I never know which fire will be entered, for that is not up to me. What is revealed and how it manifests is up to the grace and integrity of the spirit and working with the spirit is effortless.

I know it is my responsibility to take the people I work with to this wonderful place, to alleviate their suffering while they are on the earth. Every experience has a purpose and the function of pain in human nature is to make the person still enough to be receptive to spiritual energies, to drive them back to the beginning of time to link up with the spirit. Entering the earth Womb gives us the realisation that we are connected to the spirit at all times. Wherever there is any suffering, accident or trauma, the physical body is bathed in the beautiful warm light that vibrates and emanates through the physical body, neutralising pain instantaneously. This is the purpose of the spirit.

For there is no longer sufficient time for us to achieve emotional integration through counselling work as we have tried in the past, it takes too long and is too difficult to do. The pain and fear of facing it can be too great; a never ending labyrinth of undiscovered emotion and intellectual fascination and imagination, which contrives situations in life to entice and enslave you, forever keeping you from the truth.

We have left the spirit of love and in its place learned to trust in beliefs created by the mind. This is why we cannot see love's purpose for we are never present in time. We have no idea how love operates, yet we know in our daily life and relationships with people that when we feel love there is no pain. Now is the time to go beneath the suffering and let the spirit of love transform us painlessly, to trust in love once more. Only when the earth Womb is pure in each one of you does it bring forth the love into the physical world through creational birth to change circumstances for the better.

Love is always there for us, all we need to do is reconnected to the source of love, to be what we are. By not demonstrating enough love in this world without thought of self, we have cut ourselves off from that which we know ourselves to be, the love. For all love needs acknowledgement within and without. From inside our body, love the universal intelligence, rises and listens, waiting, radiating out into the world, until on the waves of recognition, it draws towards itself the right circumstances in your life for it to flow out into all life. Silent, ever vigilant to make the connection in time, redirecting our lives so that we may be fulfilled.

When we are in a state of presence with no yesterday or tomorrow, the blue flame can enter in. The synchronicity of its power is unique. When every level of consciousness in the spiritual and physical is in place, the energy of impersonal Love can flood in and what we call a miracle can take place.

My problem was trying to understand what, if anything, was required of me. I was to see the profundity of this gift later in my life; to learn, work and live with the spirit of impersonal Love was awe-inspiring and sometimes devastating as it tried to show me the meaning of truth. The Revealer eternally within me showed me the mystery of Divine Presence; the inner and outer worlds in perfect balance, pure consciousness in the moment. That is Presence that is pure Love.

Chapter x

The Cobalt Blue Flame

I did not realise that in time I was to give up the whole of myself to the point of physical death, in order to be reunited with all the fires in the earth Womb. These lit up in me gradually, as each time I descended into the earth Womb, my consciousness would be focused on a particular flame to learn and absorb the spiritual truth represented within it. I experience this as an observer with my intelligence detached from the mind. The inner spiritual world being in another dimension first reflects then moves into my feeling body, relaying the knowledge onto my mind.

When I guide others into this place some of them feel it physically and others are simply aware that something has happened. Some are overwhelmed, others feel different but can not say how, but I know through vision that radical changes have taken place. Through my Love for people I take as many there as I can.

The earth Womb has great purpose for humanity because of the purging, cleansing and forging powers of the fires, that enable us to pour out Love from our bodies into the world, forming the energy of creation. As I continue to be given the knowledge and purpose of the earth Womb, the living reality of it is demonstrated to me on the outside.

The Blue Pillar

You cannot be anything in the microcosm that you do not feel and work out in the physical body. The reality of this deep and profound knowledge is that the earth Womb is not open to everybody's awareness, and those who enter it can only see and join with the cobalt blue flame if they are truly in union with the Love energy.

Furthest away from all the other flames, standing apart in glorious omnipotence, is this blue pillar of fire, the omnipotent God energy. The flames emanating from the pillar, floods the bodies of people in the world with light and knowledge, bringing purity into the physical world. The cobalt blue flame is a very profound God energy, chemical in nature that transforms matter and is the fire I receive most from. The magnificence of the command with which it holds you is truly astounding: cosmic and spiritual beauty brought together in this reality. It holds the male and female serpent energy for the earth and cosmos, action and presence. It is activated by the opposite and released into the world only when Love is acknowledged and by God's command. It runs through the earth and cosmos and, in certain circumstances, can be activated within ones physical body.

It contains within it the spiritual essence of all people who have ever lived. It is the eternal flame that draws us towards it in unrelenting Love, extracting the essence of purity from within the physical body into the fiery blue pillar. In every one of us resides the power of the blue flame through which we can be transported back to God at any time. For most people this happens when the body has expired and for only a few during their material existence. When you reach this eternal place, you are prepared to give up your physical life to be reunited with its energy. In the profundity of the Love you feel it is a choiceless situation.

The cobalt blue flame can do all things, transform all life and resurrect the eternal bodies of everybody who has ever lived. You have no power against it for it is a dissolving energy drawing you towards it to dissolve your former self in order to live a renewed physical life on the planet in a new spiritual creation. As I look into the flames of the blue pillar of fire, I can see in each flame a diminutive figure, a golden body, representing the eternal body of each person. This is the pinnacle of God consciousness residing within you and to which you are irresistibly drawn to be reunited with God. The potency of the blue pillar provides the extra life force for the people of this earth who are in distress, calling out to omnipotent God for help.

It is there to keep your body purified, to burn away emotion and raise you above suffering. The flame can become covered by emotion and, in current times, in many people it has gone out, a wick with no flame. The blue flame is the sacred area of your divinity. It expands to protect you to deflect anything from the physical world to keep you pure.

It is a part of God in you that needs recognition, so that the divine may live through you on earth. By you giving too much to the world through your will, it can retract and be extinguished. By not taking responsibility for loving your opposite in life the Love is automatically retracted from you, passing the Love and the power to your opposite, or to where Love is greatest, regardless of your own will. Thus it is ensured that Love serves, for Love's function is to ease suffering.

This blue flame comes impersonally to each and every one of you prepared to work rightly in your life to receive it, to allow it to burn through the accumulation of the choking past. Re-igniting the blue wick and allowing it to burn freely can transform you into the godly person that you were at the beginning of time.

Such are our times that I see emotion smothering this beautiful and pure flame like a closed black flower, as dense as concrete. It is becoming increasingly difficult for people to reach the blue flame, but I know we must do so while in our physical body. There is no other time but now.

This is not an easy task but it is workable through your life experience. You can connect anytime with your eternal essence while in the physical body and know and live it. The purpose for life on this earth is so that we may pour out God's eternal body of Love into the beautiful natural world to make this earth the paradise it was before it was corrupted by the mind. This means giving up all projection of negative thought out into the world and realising the knowledge that all power is within.

Everything that leaves the body should be released in a conscious creative form. Unhappiness is caused by unconscious projection from the mind whether you know it or not. It is delusion to think that by projecting your anger and emotions outside your body, you have relieved yourself of your problems. They cannot be transformed in that way, this is only a temporary solution and the original problem will return months or years later.

Unleashing them into the world only causes more suffering for those who follow. We create the beauty of the earth, and we give emotion the life force to wreak it's will upon the earth whilst we stand back and watch in horror. The mists of emotion that emanate from us, in the form of a black veil, cause all the wars and violence upon this earth, without us even realising it.

This is where the mind never informs you rightly. The truth is that we must hold onto our negative energies such as anger, jealousy or fear and contain them within our body, not letting them out. In doing so we take full responsibility for them and they are purified within through internal combustion, often felt as heat, intense tension or explosions in the body. This gives you back the lost energy you gave up to thinking. The measure of how much you have transformed is evident by the love and peace you feel; renewed energy and enlightenment to live your life more fully. This is our responsibility in life, holding the two opposites in perfect balance. This is in our power.

The emotions of the past surface as suffering through generation after generation. It is given to us by the divine Will at birth to work through and put right, giving us the responsibility to make it conscious. But it cannot be personalised as our own: this is where we lose our way for we are all one body on this earth. The emotional energy holds you until the time of its transformation; if you are unable to transform it, it will take you to unconscious death and move on to another body reincarnating the same suffering. We have right to make others suffer. Creating immediate or long term Karma.

Everything has to return eventually to source to be transformed and purified in order to be re-united with its original God State. Once the transformation and union within has taken place, your body will be at peace; you will be able to go through death consciously and enter into the Paradise earth. The union cannot be achieved if we continually allow this overshadowing of ourselves and permit the corruption of the minds energy to be projected from the body each day. The blue flame is within you, to make the transformation painless if you can give yourself to it. It is universal intelligence in humanity.

Africa
I have seen some miraculous interactions of Love taking place in the blue flame within the body psyche. Real Love has no form, no words. It is impersonal, pure action without thought or desire. If we could live our lives through the knowledge of impersonal Love, then we would all have the joy of being

reunited. As long as you have the knowledge of the eternal flame of Love, nothing else is important. No matter what happens in life everything will be right.

With tears in her eyes, she told me her husband had been shot in Africa. She wanted to return to be near his body but was not able to enter the country again because of the uprising. She asked me if I could help her. I do not always know how the spirit will operate and on this occasion I saw the blue flame pass between us and as it reached her she slipped into a deep meditative state. The flame burned brightly in her solar area, and I saw her chest rise, her facial expression change and she appeared younger.

Then I saw a second flame touch and enfold her own. His presence in the form of a flame had joined with hers and, in a cascade of coloured light emanating from them, they began to dance in delight at the fulfilment of their union. As the dance continued light radiated through her upper body until she was completely filled with Love. He departed from her body leaving her with his Eternal Love. She was complete. I met her again several times for more sessions and she still felt they were together and never had the desire to return to Africa again.

Chapter xi

The Green Flame

The green flame is female bringing all nature through her body. It is the movement of her true feeling body of Love inside the physical body. The body that moves in man and woman and in which is felt their Love of nature, Love of spirit and Love of the opposite, man and woman.

The whole of the world is suffused in this magnificent energy. As I moved closer and closer to the pure Love of the creator, my body was engulfed by these waves of spiritual energy from all of nature. On walks in the countryside I would feel the energy form into a beautiful green flame, which danced around me and blended into my body, incorporating within it the energy of nature. This is the feeling of Love returned to source, where Mother earth has become one with you in the fluid state of natural energy.

To contain this Paradise within, by meeting your eternal spirit on the inside, is often not possible in the physical world because we have forgotten how to truly love and many people are distressed. This fluid state of being within has a deep and profound purpose to connect the loved one to their true nature. I have worked with many to reconnect the flow into their physical body. Forever present, the spirit of God will come to you in the sacred place within the body reserved for Love.

As I was being shown more and more through my daily life, the centre of all spiritual Love is in the physical body and I set about working to help all men and women realise this knowledge. This energy can link you to your opposite, before and after death, and remain in your spirit body for eternity. If you give back to the earth what she gave to you then mother Earth will serve you in the body. To be given these energies is indeed a precious thing and has to be realised in this existence, here and now in the body and treated, nurtured and loved properly.

This manifestation of the union that is woman and man can happen at any time. It is part of the pure psychic and mental state of mind and body as they become cleansed. For this to happen the mind has to be filled with the power of the spirit of Love. When the spirit enters the mind it is trying to tell you and to show you what you really are; there is no choice but to go with it, the mind becomes filled with the creation. I have no control over these experiences when they begin, but I am looked after throughout and always return to the physical world through my body.

With all the mental and spiritual cleansing and energising and working with people the Love became greater and the union within me deeper.

The Cat

She felt increasingly at one with all things. She saw the beautiful green flame more and more and felt nature within her body. She was idly sitting one afternoon, stroking a beautiful cat on her lap taking in the joy of everything around her. She felt the presence of the spirit of God, and the profound stillness as everything stopped in time. She felt again nature move within, her attention was brought down into her body and she became one with the beautiful animal. The intelligence within becoming one with nature and she began to move through the starry universe.

She was pulled around inside her body in a great kaleidoscope of energy, a figure of eight movement drawing heaven and earth together, the matrix of all life. Scanning the matrix she could see star systems coming together, colliding and releasing huge waves of cosmic energy; and every animal that was ever born, every seed, every tree, all of life; every instance of awakening in every animal and every expiring too. All the way back in time to when we were amphibians, dinosaurs and flying creatures. All the creations that have ever been on this earth, all of life was opened up to her.

As each colour of the spectrum opened up before her within the matrix, the sun and moon dancing in the universe would spontaneously reveal great truths of the creation on this earth. She saw all the myriad body forms that have had life, unrecognisable until looking into their eyes. She had that unmistakable feeling of being with a loved one, the reflection of the intelligence and consciousness that runs through all life, within and without. A knowing that never changes. And so through this animal God revealed another aspect of impersonal Love, for God in nature can do anything, anywhere, anytime.

The Amphibian

This vision brought me to a deeper understanding of why people have their differences. I was talking to a student during a session when she transformed into an amphibian as I spoke. She began to breathe through cheek gills and her body changed into scaled armour. I could see the whole of the wondrous natural world within her, a beauty that we do not see today. There followed a session with her husband and as I looked at him he changed into a flying creature akin to a pterodactyl. They had been two distinctly separate species in a different creation on this earth and I realised that this could be the cause of their problems on a deeper level.

I spoke to them together and took them back into the spiritual world where they could experience this for themselves. And there under the sun in the solar centre I saw a union take place between them. After this session, their life together began to change for the better.

The Revealer came in a flash of brightly coloured vortices dancing in front of me until He came to a halt and stepped forward. I could see the magnificence of His spirit form. He talked to me of my vision telling me this was pure memory of all time showing me the different bodies that we have in different creations. The human mind can only see us as human, but in the whole of the creations we are many different species behind the human form. We cannot see anything original beyond this lifetime for in this creation there is only partial emotional memory of past lives within our present body. But people personalise emotional memory, thinking it their own past experience and try to understand its meaning.

Nature Spirits

She was tending her garden when she was filled with the power of the earth spirit. The pure spiritual psychic energy of nature formed from the energy of all the trees, flowers and grass, which in its pure form is Love. It swirled around her like a great vortex and she knew she was becoming one with all things. The earth was changing before her very eyes. She felt a leaf transform into billions of angels unfolding to flow and dance into delicate oscillations of light. And she felt her body vibrate and the little angels flew around and in and through her body, vibrating with it on the same wavelength as nature.

Every time I went into the garden I would get the same wonderful effect on my body and mind. A oneness with everything that was clearing my mind, leaving it cleansed and transformed. Mother nature yielding all her energies into the trees, into the birds, and my body was beginning to flow with this same unique fluid energy as my mind was becoming one with all life. I could hear the rustling of the trees and the wind blowing in my body, Mother Nature in communication. A flower would open, a seed would burst, a grain of earth give nourishment. I felt at one with everything from inside my body, I had internalised natural energy. I was in nature behind form within, and in nature in form on the outside, the two perfectly balanced. The balance is imperative to hold the body together at this stage, otherwise man and woman can die into this form of impersonal Love for they are all nature.

A Tiny Miracle

Just before Christmas the same year, I was holding a workshop at home. There were eight people attending and it was very cold, with the temperature below zero. The first thing we did was to honour Mother earth by singing earth songs thanking her for all she does and I kept seeing, throughout the morning, the vision of a wonderful metamorphosis from a chrysalis taking place. It was something I did not quite understand, but later in the day the meaning of it was revealed.

As dusk fell we held a candlelit ceremony and felt the beauty of nature rushing into us and embracing us, even in the house. As we closed our eyes again to thank Mother Nature for the abundance of the earth I heard the flapping of tiny wings and I felt it in my body. A beautiful natural Love filled us all and around the candles there danced a butterfly. It flew from one knee to another as we sat cross-legged on the floor. The wonder of its tiny wings, the profusion of bright colours, and its complete and absolute knowing of life filled us with great joy. It was so overwhelming it brought us into oneness.

After we had acknowledged it we knew it had to be freed. Although outside in the cold it would die we knew it needed to go back to nature to demonstrate our union with nature, so we let it go.

The Hurricane

Walking in woodland she could feel the bark and leaves of the trees becoming liquid energy, blending with her own body. And she could hear the birds singing the song of creation and the sound of it oscillated with all of nature around her in the magnificent oneness of life. And the sun shone like billions of golden angels circling around every tree and flower and every blade of grass until all merged into a wonderful harmony and balance. At night, the moon danced on the water and all around she could hear the birds, the bats, all nightlife combines into one harmonious song.

When the weather changed she could see every raindrop, like millions of tiny crystals, burst into beautiful, incandescent, multicoloured prisms of light when they hit the ground. During a storm she could see tiny spirals of energy coming towards her in formation drawing behind them the larger vortices of the wind. Out in the starry universe she saw an impending hurricane, the essence of it beginning deep in space and building power. With her universal consciousness now developed, through the very eye of the storm she could see the south of England and two days later the hurricane swept across our land, felling hundreds of trees and leaving a trail of devastation in its path.

In this way nature and I became one and I came to realise these same energies suffused and incorporated the whole of the universe. Mentally I was losing my ability to hold together the material world. Objects would de-materialise before my very eyes and I knew then that nothing was solid in this world, absolutely nothing. As I walked towards things they would disappear and reform as I walked past. Even my own body blended with nature to the point of dematerialisation. It is very hard to retain material reality when you are shown the incredible beauty of the earth and spirit because it becomes you and you become it. At times I would long to become it permanently, to blend with it totally and to be free of the mind that pressed on me. But I was not allowed to die into it permanently, nature was not ready for me yet. I wondered why the spirit of Love was giving me such beauty, and what was I to do after becoming one with it.

Merging Energies

As I travelled through the spiritual realms, beyond the formation of our world, listening to this sound of the universe singing its wonderful song, I was at one with all things and I began to experience this with the people around me. The beautiful flow of energy through their body would oscillate with mine, and as I looked, their physical body would dissolve to reveal their energies merging with nature. Some were drawn to flowers, others to water, trees or animals. The energies of those that had fulfilled their natural task on the earth and were near the end of their life no longer emanated energy from their body, for they had become the earth. No longer had they need to be on the earth having given their eternal blessing into the earth through their life.

In my vision of the consciousness behind time, I see the beauty of the earth, in its atomic form, emanating from each individual's body out through the solar plexus to create the outer kingdom, which we know as nature. As this pours out of their bodies I have a wonderful pure psychic vision of the conjoined psychic and spiritual energy, which I see transformed into the most breathtaking and spontaneous natural and loving interaction in the natural world. People produce different things in the universe, contributing to the creation and earth's evolution without even realising it. They manifest in the outer world the reality of the beauty within themselves, pouring it out of their very being. In vision I sense the manifestation of it and I am swamped by the beauty of the life around me.

The function of the brain is to resonate with these energies from the solar plexus. It superimposes onto them a vibrating substance, which forms them into everything in nature. This is how the physical world is being kept alive from moment to moment. In the sacred lands there is no decay, everything keeps its pristine beauty and stays as pure as it ever was. This is what you return to after physical death, back into this energy. It is this pure psychic and spiritual energy I help people to connect with.

At times I wondered if I would survive this wonderful knowledge and how I was to hold my body together. It felt like I was dying into the earth. The Revealer came through the angelic spirits of nature to assure me all was well. The work had already started on holding my physical form together and He said He would show me more when I was ready to receive the next step of the spiritual knowledge.

Chapter xii

Healing the Mind

The earth Womb and Tomb is the one and only place where the last form of any knowledgeable imprint on the mind can take place. When its energy comes up into the mind it wipes out all negative memory. This is when the two spiritual principles of all life, God or the Goddess, enter the mind transforming and filling it with the creation. Indeed love is the greatest and most perfect way of entering into this place. Love has no opposite polarities and its action is only to serve. Waiting patiently to show you the truth of what you are, rushing forth to fill those who can accept it.

I cannot enter the earth Womb with any mental concept or by any physical exertion. Becoming the observer, I focus my consciousness on my fluid feeling body inside my physical form. By its very nature of fluid movement and freedom from fixed form, my consciousness bypasses the mind with its fixed mental images and emotions and moves into this beautiful sacred place, allowing clear access into the spiritual realms, where I am now.

Allow Love Access

Allow yourself to become eternal while you are alive. By being connected to the blue flame at all times you will achieve death consciously, before it seeks you out. You will find the road home and be helped all along the way. There is nothing that the spirit will not do for you if you allow Love to have access to you at all times.

Love purifies all suffering from within, giving you the power to further your spiritual evolution while in a body, to enter the Paradise on earth before death. It keeps you conscious through the death so that you never know death's sting. Your mantle, the body falls away and your beautiful spiritual body of golden essence takes its place in nature and walks free of all restraint, giving you your Paradise now.

Moving through the death band by the action of Love is just like going to sleep consciously. Only fear gets in the way. The black veil of the minds own fear sets up a barrier through which you cannot pass and progress. It holds you prisoner gripping your attention tenaciously so it can impose its own small world of limited reality and its unnatural pressures on your body, for it knows one day it will die. It is not natural, for nature does not come from that part of the mind.

If you feel the need to release yourself from the mind's imprisonment, meditate on the blue flame to lead you down to the safe area within your body, behind emotion. There, no longer controlled by the mind, your awareness becomes the observer entering the feeling body and moving into the sacred space where you feel warm, safe and at peace within. There you can only manifest love and peace. Goodness of the mind is self serving, always coinciding with its own objectives for self gratification. Goodness of the body where true consciousness resides is the manifestation of the true earth spirit of love, which serves the creation ceaselessly.

Transforming Past Energies
Once you have reclaimed the areas of your psychic and emotional body and transformed the sickness and mental chaos into this wonderful flame energy. You will have all the energy you need spiritually to empower you to move into the spiritual realms, to make your descent home whilst staying alive in the physical body. To know this and bring it out into

the physical earth, to divine it from your very being, is the very purpose of your life now. Why remain on the surface of yourself when you can enter deep within your sacred space, your spiritual consciousness, the earth Womb, the earth's core and be united with the whole of life.

When you have transformed past energy you feel it in the body as lightness and peace, your mental, physical and emotional suffering returned back into pure energy. And this interaction with the spirit gives you more fuel to descend even deeper and the power of the spirit will be revealed to you to empower you.

The earth Womb is a place of passing through, where everything comes together and everything is harmonised. There is much work to do, as you move down through each level. The spirit of truth, the blue flame, will be with you, giving you safe passage through the psychic death band and placing you unconditionally in the spirit realms, painlessly. The fluid body will do the rest, cleansing you of past as you move deep into your being. It is time to draw the earth's power back into our sacred place, the earth Womb within us, to nourish our spiritual being and bring more Love into our physical bodies, which in turn will nourish the earth for eternity.

Balancing Opposites

The mind in its transformed state then becomes a magnificent instrument used by the spirit of the divine mind to enhance life on the physical earth every day. Your situation in life improves and you radiate your being to all those around you in Love and peace. This is the power of the spirit, the nucleus of which is within you in the form of the sun centre, which has to be linked up with its opposite the moon, also within your body, reflected in the cosmos by the sun and moon.

All levels can be interfaced with all opposites as we descend down through the levels of mind and emotion and deeper into the psyche, through the levels beyond physical death and into the power of the spirit. But first we have to let go of the gripping mind that will always hold you as a servant because it cannot know the power of the spirit of Love. The coloured flames are the means to hold and interface all opposites to give you passage through the varied vibrations of each spiritual realm.

The Computer Mind

In its ignorance the mind thinks it is all there is, that it controls the natural world. But in reality it is a computer with a limited programme that only registers the progress of the material world with no reference to the totality of the natural world. Indeed the world is constructed by the mind, but it is built on the Womb of the earth, the Womb of woman, which it cannot enter or know. For the earth Womb can not be entered through the mind, only through Love. When honouring love first, it automatically takes command in your life and the transition becomes easier.

When Love enters the mind it has complete command, transforming it in the first instance into the utter shock of complete nothingness. With nothing to hold onto, a feeling of loss and breaking of all ties is realised. But accompanied by the feeling and knowledge within of the supreme peace and beauty of the union with all life. The point of perfection is held for short periods in timeless union, as the mind becomes accustomed to the purity and space before being filled again with our world.

When all this is realised by your understanding and consciousness, you will then be able to descend deeper into the other realms of consciousness that I speak of; and die to the world and enter into the earth Womb in full consciousness, for its beauty surpasses all. Then you will no longer suffer through the mind and you will be linked to that which is the truth now, seeing all things, all worlds, all of life suffused together. You become at one with the whole of life now, which radiates and emanates through your body as the nucleus of Love incarnate on this earth.

Death

I have entered the many realms of the sacred spirit that open up to those who seek in truth, where I was informed of all aspects of spiritual consciousness, the understanding of life that is before birth and after death. I realised on my journey into the earth Womb and Tomb, the world of harmony and balance, that beyond the depths of the subconscious mind there is no death. We are all united and eternal.

Your spiritual twin, your psychic body, is the means for you to realise this amazing truth. This body, which never dies, ensures your link with the eternal is forever secured. My spirit twin directed and guided me to my eternal love beyond death, channelling the love back through my mind and body. Switching my attention from the controlling mind to that of the conscious observer, it was possible to be with my permanent spirit body as it led me through the spirit realms. In my descent into this place I encountered many levels of consciousness, beyond the limited reality of the brain and mind. The brain and the mind die along with the physical body, but we have within us this ever-present spirit of life, pure consciousness, which continues and manifests here on earth after the body has expired.

We make consciousness, by the love we have for each other; this is why the concept of consciousness is so difficult to understand. The purpose of conscious is to support the creation. Consciousness then informs you of your eternal life, given to you as, pure knowledge, which is unparalleled. This is your pure memory, that which you never lose from creation to creation. Emotional memory that appears to live on after your death is short-lived and only accessible in these times.

You, as people of the earth spirit, will want to become one with this spirit of truth, to become universally conscious. To have the knowledge of what is happening in the whole earth and cosmos and consciously take part in it. For you are the earth spirit, sustained by the ever present, vibrant substance of God in the cosmos and in nature all around in the form of universal impersonal Love. Manifested through the body of man and woman in Love.

The mind has drawn us so far away from our Love and loved ones. It is only the mind that blocks us from this reality and if we consciously enter into our body, for all is in there, the beauty will be made manifest each day. I learned we do not ever leave our body, everything happens within. It is only the mind that projects the experience outside. All energy has to come into the body to be cleansed, not the other way round.

If you can offer yourself to the still centre of Love, suffering will be swept away and a joy will flood in bringing you infinite peace. This is the law of the Great Spirit of Love. If you stay with it, it will always serve you, suffusing all that you are as you descend down into the beautiful serene place of harmony and balance. Prepared and purified for your eternal earth spirit.

Chapter xiii

The Purified Mind

I saw that there is more to the earth Womb than just the spiritual fires. It transforms and enlightens man and woman's mind, but they have to be prepared to give themselves up to its greater power. Although the mind can eventually be mastered it usually comes through crisis or trauma as happened to me. This is often the only way the mind can be shocked and cleansed of the past and thus purified.

If you do not willingly open yourself to the truth of the universe, life or God has their way of dealing with you to make sure that you are reunited. I have known some people who in their trust of the earth Womb have put themselves absolutely and completely into the hands of the spiritual fire thus allowing it to work out in their bodies. To purify the mind and body in this way is by far the quickest, easiest, and least painful of all. It heals by dissolving past pain, which then registers on the mind and body the beauty of Creation. Sometimes seeing angels is a measure of its purity, transporting you into the sacred lands. This union of mind and body serves you to the highest degree.

In the physical world this means ridding your self of selfishness and working through the transformed mind of Love which serves the creation without thought of self. It means changes in your life, which can be unsettling and traumatic, but it becomes a lot easier as you allow the higher power to take over and show you the way. This can be a difficult concept for the mind to grasp, but once the mind experiences it there is no going back for truly the reunification with the God energy, to make man and woman living Gods, is all the mind needs and wants.

The Black Flame of the Impersonal Mind

The black flame that burns in the earth Womb is the part of the mind that through selfish desire can enter the physical world to become a corrupt, malevolent shadow manifesting as violence, avarice and errant sexual and mental force. When retracted back into its God state and kept in control and equilibrium, it returns back to its purified state of pure Love. The mind is purified and made impersonal, through death of the self, of emotion. It then comes under the control of the divine power that resides in the earth Womb and is very powerful. The beauty that is shown to you highlights the wrongs the wilful mind has imposed on your life, giving you time to put them right in your own experience.

Once the black energy and all its desires are contained, the mind and Love come together. Love is in union. The union takes place in the body in the figure of eight movement between the heart and the head, and the pure and absolute balance of one giving to the other is realised. Love flows into the mind, cleansing it and universal Love is compacted within the body. This manifests physically as a feeling of profound uplifting, total union with the consciousness of all life on earth and in the cosmos through the physical body on earth.

The Black-red Flame of Subconscious Cleansing

The Black-red flame is particularly fascinating because it deals with subconscious entities permanently and effectively. Many of you working in a spiritual context understand this is a very difficult area to cleanse. As you open the door spiritually, entities can rush through taking hold of the mind, keeping the person from Love, which can take a lifetime to purify. This is the flame that absorbs the emotional entities from the subconscious where they are consumed in the fire.

Another of its qualities is aiding cell regeneration. For a new body to be created, it first has to be taken from the matter currently in your own physical body. In this emotional mass are sparks of conscious energy, which can be built up sufficiently to create a flame bringing new cells to life. In this flame the old subconscious patterning is purified and eliminated so that the regeneration can then take place.

The Pink Flame of Innocent Love

Everything is an extraction of the purity of life, suffering and pain is a distortion of it. When transformed it is returned and reunited with its original energy. This is how new energy is transfused to its right place in the physical body, reclaiming what is already yours. But it takes Love, gentleness and kindness and recognition of the whole, for awareness of the parts only causes more suffering. It is mostly females who enter this flame.

She felt a flame burning in her chest and a great surge of energy run through her body. She realised the child within her was looking out, searching and hovering above the earth Womb with angels. She looked down at the cowled forms and the fires in the earth Womb, uncertain which one to choose. Then the angels surrounded her and led her down to the pink fire and the flames gently enveloped her. And all the past suffering, which had attached itself to her as a young child and remained there ever since, was consumed in their flaming caress.

The force of the world in her, the sexual snake carried since birth within her body or put there when still a child was transformed, returning her back to the state of innocent Love.

Now she was sufficiently mature to understand the significance of integrating it back into the pure energy of innocent Love. For woman can only carry innocent purified love when she is sufficiently mature and experienced to keep it from corruption.

The energy swept through her and the pink flame steadily grew until it now burned in her body as a living reality of the truth that all things in us can be healed if we know how to bring the energy of past suffering into the power of the present. For in the present there is only renewal. The flame is the presence of God that knows no end and is waiting behind time in the sacred worlds for your return.

Barcelona

Whilst the mind is being purified it can be an extremely traumatic experience before you are united with all life. As the mind vainly tries to retain its grip on you it creates psychic phenomena to engage your attention.

One morning I awoke abruptly from a nightmare, which I was to discover later, was a premonition. Although I had already had several small premonitions in the past, this surpassed them in intensity and clarity. Seeing how shaken I was my husband was concerned. I had seen a large campsite in a hot, sunny country with a happy holiday atmosphere associated with the place. Suddenly there was a gigantic explosion followed by several smaller ones leaving charred and burned bodies strewn everywhere.

I woke the next morning with exactly the same premonition but this time I was on a hill looking down at the disaster below. As I was telling my friend Anne at work about the recurrence of the nightmare we heard a report on the radio about a disaster in Barcelona. An oil tanker had skidded off the road by a campsite and burst into flames, igniting in turn the campers gas bottles, creating a huge fireball. The death toll, they said, was unknown but could run into hundreds.

Ann ran from the room crying that her husband and four children were on holiday at that resort. She could not get a reply for a long while from the British Embassy but finally, her family was reported safe. Ann's family had taken photos of the disaster and the scene was exactly as I had seen it in my premonition.

This was my mind trying to hold my attention by thrusting the past into the present. The reality had already taken place within my mind and the mind of all people. As the Love in me grew stronger the grip of the mind became more powerful and I had many such experiences. I did not want to live like this, it was all far too traumatic, but how to stop it was the main question. Then I was shown that the consciousness of Love has power over the mind and can put the mind to rest.

City Rush Hour

One day I was caught up in a city traffic jam, wishing I had chosen a better time than the rush hour to travel, when I was thrust into the psyche. I saw before me a tropical beach with the sun shining down on the sea. I drove for miles across the sand between palm trees and then the vision receded. Returning to reality I found myself safely across the other side of the city and on my way home. This vision demonstrated to me how consciousness has ultimate control of the situation and safeguard of the body, over-riding the mind.

Chapter xiv

The Solar Centre

She could see a swirling black vortex of externalised emotion pressing down on the top of her head. The pineal gland swelled to a large conical shape to accommodate the emotional energy and drew it down into the diaphragm to where the blue flame burns, where it was consumed.

When you become one with the solar centre, the emotion you have projected outside is drawn back into the body for integration to take place. The pineal gland in the centre of the head opens up to whatever size is needed to suck in the errant emotional energy and deep and profound healing can then take place.

The consciousness was showing me how to deal with the emotion that slips out of us unconsciously. We have no understanding of how we contribute to the suffering of the world through the thinking mind. We are made to live what we create, but it can not be personalised, for we are a part of all life and we share the responsibility of making conscious the ignorance of the past as a whole.

Descending down to my solar centre for healing to transform the emotion was to be a regular occurrence in my life. I became practised at controlling my troublesome mind by being very still, conscious of the moment, enabling me to bypass it, not allowing it to draw me back into the past. Integration of all emotion and projected energies automatically takes place when one is still enough.

As I reintegrated these mental energies and ceased to focus on the Barcelona experience I went deeper into my body. I could see within there were sparks of living mind energy, leftover from the powerful psychic manifestation of premonition, and it seemed that this energy, like a beacon, was leading me deeper into my being. It led me beyond the earth Womb to a place of warmth and an intense feeling of safety.

The Sun Spot

She became aware of an intensely bright light inside her head like an internal sun, an inescapable focus of attention moving down through her body. Her body felt no longer part of her, and she was in another world where the sun shone from a cloudless sky onto a golden sandy beach. The heat in her body was tremendous, everything became clearer and more distinct and she experienced a great sense of calmness. She was in the solar centre within, a safe haven while healing was carried out on her body.

Moving into the sun centre is of particular significance, because the sun can project you further and deeper into the body, into the inner universe itself. It is the place of spiritual union. It heals the body by the release of solar atoms, which activate healing and reprograms the atoms in the body producing an intense physical heat, clearing blocked energies painlessly and bringing about the most remarkable realisations within you. It has to be done gradually for it is so powerful.

Drawing her deeper beneath the sun, a thread was released from the sun centre to form a breathtaking golden cord of angels spiralling up towards her, enveloping her spiritual body. An offering of grace to her, she had reached the centre of her body, she had united with the God within. She could bring this golden cord back into the mind in the physical world giving her clear access in and out of the solar plexus to God at all times.

For some people this does not happen and I have to lead them back there repeatedly. This continues the gradual transformation of the body and mind and it can take years to go through the process properly. As I see this union of solar plexus and mind consciousness coming together in people it brings me great joy. There is nothing greater than taking someone to the Love or God within. To enable them to further themselves spiritually, taking them from the solar plexus down into the world of the deep psyche; the sacred place of mystery with God.

Chapter xv

The Magenta Violet Flame of Spiritual and Physical Union

The flames in the earth Womb all work to bring us into union with the opposite. The magenta violet flame can in some situations unite us with the opposite on the physical level, the union of man and woman in world. It is my joy to lead people into this flame to experience this union.

The cowled forms came out of the fire adorned in purple robes, a splendid sight. They stepped forward to make an archway with their fiery swords held high to guide her through into the centre of the flame. She became weightless, floating as the flickering and caressing flame enveloped her spiritual body. The cowled forms formed a circle around the flame touching it with their fiery swords. In acknowledgement the flame flashed out to the swords and the energy of it tingled scintillatingly through her body.

She saw a man being led through the archway from the physical world into the fire. He stepped into the flame to join with her in perfect union of male with female. With the flames lapping around them there was a beautiful outpouring of Love and celebration and joyfulness from the cowled forms encircled around them.

This flame is where the union takes place in the physical as well as in the spiritual, where the man is fused to woman in the spiritual flame so he can serve her in the physical world. It is an inner marriage that can also be impersonal. If it is not acknowledge by the opposite in the physical world then the Love can be made on the spiritual plane and felt in the body, I have seen this many times.

A couple came to me who could not consummate their Love. In vision I saw the man prepare a place of beauty for his woman, a bed of flowers with candles burning all around and she would go there and wait for him to come to Love her. Thus their Love was made spiritually and they could then sense the feeling of this Love come through into their physical bodies. This is sometimes necessary to keep love pure.

In the material world and the physical world we must serve each other in the understanding of the importance of giving Love to another before we can receive it. No truth can be realised without the essence of Love being passed from one to the other in service of the other. Spiritual Love will only find its way to those people who use it rightly. This is Love's greatest mystery and strength, ensuring Love will not be abused; Love's integrity. And all truth, from any mind, comes from the power of Love entering it.

The Permanent Body

The permanent body is the indestructible body behind time working impersonally to transport Love to the beloved ones. It has the power to bestow freedom through Love to relieve those suffering, by bringing about union in all situations of separation. The permanent body linked together with the spiritual flames between two worlds is the custodian of Love.

The Revealer showed me how to take my Love to people. I enter into one of the many flames in the Womb and then carry a portion of the Love in my energy body and drop it into the upper body of the loved one. Sometimes people see me come to them at night to put a glow around them; or visit them in an animal or bird form they recognised as me, to take them through the archway of spiritual flames and drop the flame of Love into their body.

Paul

One of my students, Paul, with whom I had been working for well over a year, was awakened to Love in a profound way. One night he awoke to see me before him.

She led him through an archway of flowers and flames to a beautiful place, the inner sacred land where the sun was shining. In the distance was something sparkling like glass, which he felt strongly drawn to. She walked with him toward it past pools of water lilies, symbolic of the female body, an indication of what was to come.

Nearing the sparkling light, he turned to her questioningly and she led him over as he looked towards it longingly. There on the grass was a glass case containing the body of a beautiful woman and he knelt down by the woman's side. His presence awakened her and her eyelids started to open. As he placed his hand on the glass case it melted and he lifted her up tenderly and held her to him. With the moment of recognition and union he bonded with the pure feeling of his spiritual Love, the awakening of the female earth spirit inside his body psyche.

I have seen many different beautiful awakenings in the men and women I have worked with, bringing them to union and equilibrium in Love, the untainted purity of Love that is always inside the body. And this is what gives rise to and eventually leads to the golden body and the passion of Love.

After working with him for a whole year, Paul went into the passion inside his body and since then it has been a great pleasure to see it manifesting on the outside in his life. As a young man he had many difficulties in life and had remained a bachelor with little experience of Love. On reaching the passion within in his early fifties he drew to him a woman, and he is now serving her in Love.

Matthew and the Sexual Snake

I began to work with people in the same ways that I was being shown, with remarkable results. One of my students, Matthew whom I had been teaching for several months, requested to be purified of his sexual energy so that he could fully love women. His powerful sex drive prevented him from loving them properly. I lead him into the solar centre where I could see the sexual snake slithering along a sandy beach; the corrupted energy of the serpent that rises into the mind, distorting our perception of life and Love.

As he disconnected from the mind he saw the snake. A great pressure built up within him and he began to perspire. Suddenly a beam of light shone from the sun centre directly onto the snake containing it and a deep voice boomed, "There is nowhere for you to hide". The snake became frantic, hissing and thrashing about in a desperate attempt to avoid the light, but there was no escape. Its skin began to scorch until it burst into flames and was consumed by the fire.

Matthew was astonished at the power of the experience and felt slightly nauseous. I suggested he should go home and be still until the feeling passed. Several days later he contacted me to say that after the initial discomfort a feeling of well being had swept over him which was still with him. I could see he had closed a chapter of his life and now things would change for the better. For everyone has to live what they become inside on the outside. When activated in the body the sun centre is the means to release the divine spark of life and Love in the physical body through lovemaking.

The next time I heard from Matthew was on his return from a holiday at a spiritual retreat. There he met a lady to whom he felt strongly attracted and who confided in him that she was a virgin although now in her forties. She felt that it was time for her to experience lovemaking and asked Matthew to help her. Although they spent several nights together he said he could not bring himself to love her.

Even after being purified and then receiving his mirror in the world it was too difficult for him. He allowed his mind to make decisions about his Love instead of trusting in life and the instinctive feelings of his body. For the body knows all things and is where the master of Love resides. And so he turned aside the opportunity God had presented to him to bring Love into this world through pure woman.

The snake is the world in man and man in woman, and is the bane of our lives; it separates us from Love. It is part of the material world which man can cope with better than woman. For her it is more troublesome, linked to her sex drive it gives her no peace, preventing her from reaching the Love without which she is lost. When removed in both man and woman a great sense of equilibrium and completeness is realised and without the distraction, the Love can be reached and the mind purified.

The Laws of Life

Impersonal spiritual Love is the most powerful love on this earth. If you wish to take responsibility for your life, you will be under the power of its action of universal law, which will operate in you to show you how to deal with life's circumstances. Keeping your mind pure to accommodate this energy is not easy, as I was to learn. The sexual force around us in the world is still linked to mind and it is a real danger, which you must be aware of at all times. Throughout my life and spiritual development the earth Womb serves to protect

me. At one time in my life I was with a group of people and I could feel there was something very wrong and forceful around me, but I knew not what. I went into vision.

The Dove and the Snake

She was whipped back into the earth Womb, the psyche, and felt within her a surge of energy so powerful she thought she would explode. She saw a snake. It had penetrated the veil, the entrance to the Womb, the place of harmony and balance and was trying to force its way into the fires. She realised the snake was the projection of the sexual force of the people around her. As one, the cowled forms turned towards it and a dove, the spirit of life, flew out of the fire and swooped down over the spitting and hissing snake. With unrelenting power, the dove circling the snake and the cowled forms, their robes sweeping the ground making no room for escape, began to drive the snake back out through the veil. She could hear it hissing and spitting outside, then the light surrounded it and it was dissolved.

I was acutely aware that this snake is the same snake of self, serving self will that entered the garden of Love at the beginning of time. The Revealer came to me in a flash of light, telling me this snake was coming from a woman and I was made aware that woman has become as forceful as man in this life.

This cannot happen in the world of Love. I wondered why the snake was dissolved and not transformed. The Revealer explained that the snake's energy of sexual force and the mind was seeking union with the divine Love it desired but could not have, for nothing can be purified by the force of violence and wanting. The great circle of fire, the earth Womb can only be entered by Love. And I realised the earth Womb really was the place of harmony and balance for all things.

Chapter xvi

Woman's Mystery

The Pure Feeling Body

The pure feeling body is a fluid function, a living intelligence that we need to keep us in contact with the spiritual essence of our body in creation. It is the mysterious, unseen knowledge, the web of all life that flows in substances throughout the earth: the rising sap in trees and grass, circulating blood, male semen to name a few. This is how the goddess moves through her creation from the spiritual worlds into our bodies and finally into our world. It can also be connected to the body through the power of the moon.

This intelligence is passed through the mother's milk as she nurtures and breast-feeds her young. It enables the baby child to be at peace when away from the mother in the comfort and knowledge of the mother's pure feeling of Love flowing through the veins and secretions of its body, the connection throughout the natural world and back through the mother.

This pure feeling energy is unique for it is the means, in the first instance, that pulls two people together magnetically to unite in Love and to take them deeper into the body of divine Love, maintaining the eternal flow of divine Love through woman's Womb into nature. The feeling of it draws them together, an undeniable recognition in the physical body. No meditation is ever needed where Love is. This feeling energy is the effortless way of connecting to the spirit of Love in all life and on all levels.

Once linked to the mental body, this intelligence moves around the body transporting the person's consciousness to different spheres of awareness effortlessly. Consciousness in its pure form is Love and knowledge, which the person will experience in their feeling body when the time is right. Being in the physical and spiritual worlds at once myself, I can help people by drawing the experience back up through their feeling body and relaying it in vision through the pure mind, making it a conscious living reality.

Some people are suffering through not being linked to this feeling, by not being breast fed, or incomplete bonding or lack of Love during nurturing as well as adult life. They can be taken to an area of the psyche where this connection is possible; where they experience freedom to flow with the spiritual energy and subsequently feel great changes within themselves.

In these times the natural cycle of life has been depleted through neglect of Love in all areas. Love properly honoured through nurturing and physical lovemaking creates and maintains the flow of spiritual and divine Love throughout the earth.

The Crystal Flame

The Crystal Flame is a scintillating magnificent flame, like a prism of light it dances continuously. It is a porthole into the chambers beneath the earth Womb. Its purpose is induction into the female energy with God. The flame is not visible, even in spiritual vision. It is one of those mysterious works of the spirit where you have to be engaged in the energy for the purpose represented in this flame and it will not reveal itself until you are ready and prepared. I guide many women into this flame when the time is right.

She descended into the earth Womb to be ceremonially prepared. At the entrance to the chamber she was met and guided by the cowled forms to a place of great beauty. Her body was clothed in a flowing iridescent gown and she was guided to where the crystal flame burns and enveloped in its beauty. She could feel the energy resonating and glistening throughout her consciousness and with the flaming caresses, her spiritual body yielded and prisms of light sparkled forth from it. Consumed in the crystalline structure of the flame, distilled into a magnificent shimmering energy with stars for eyes, she experienced a deep feeling of the female, which she instinctively recognised.

The cowled forms then led her to a lower chamber in the earth Womb. Entering this still place she was escorted to an altar of crystal and pure gold. Lifting her spirit body, they lowered her into the centre, where the pure feeling of the female had been stored and kept safe for her return. Rising from this vital liquid, the cowled forms ceremoniously lowered the veil of purity over her head to protect her before her re-entry into the physical world. She felt magnificent, completely at one, united with her own wondrous female energy.

As this energy works through the physical body the woman feels peace and serenity, a pureness and cleansing. All tension drops from the mind, mental suffering is eased and all thinking ceases. She simply becomes the female energy. This is not easy to define; it is a movement within the great body of the earth Womb, a liquid energy that only appears at certain times. As the spirit pauses there she feels it with a unique knowing, an enhancement of the spiritual essence of the female, a mystery that she alone can understand and work with.

Entering this liquid energy she is compelled to move with the rhythm of life, with nature and the seasons, birth and death, the cosmic sun and the moon, the mystery of feeling through flowing waters, the pull of tides and the spirit of air. She is able to move into these areas at all times to fulfil any task that is asked of her on this earth, through the Love of the opposite, through the solar male. Any man around her sympathetic to these feelings will enhance her life and, needless to say, such a man is usually brought into her orbit so that she may have the chance to live this beautiful energy in the physical world.

The earth Womb creates all life and also the power to flush out and purify the world of emotion in woman through the lunar cycle of the Womb. Far from being the curse women may think, it is indeed a blessing. It is the emotion that attaches itself to the menses that is the curse. Woman should use this time of her cycle to get in touch with herself in the knowledge that she is separating and being freed from the emotion. It is a natural and beautiful process and without it there would be far more suffering. Once purified, the blood can become sacred again.

The spiritual energy and the female energy never ever fail you. Life always presents the opportunity for you to live this energy to the full. Once entered there is no going back, for you have left the world and gone into the mysterious journey of no end. I look forward to taking as many women as possible into this place and I have seen the results working in life. Whether the woman is single or with a partner, the enhancement to life is positive and very necessary to bring Love back to its rightful place here on the earth.

The Animal Womb

Another unique aspect of the solar plexus is its link to the Womb in the figure eight movement. For some people entering within there night can fall, making it possible to enter into the pure side of woman, the mystery of Mother earth. The darkness and the mystique, the origin of all life comes from out of woman's body through her Womb. It is the yin energy and it can be reached by woman through the moon when her body vibration is speeded up sufficiently to link with the lunar energy. Then she can enter the beautiful, velvety darkness of the inner worlds, like coming home, as everything unfolds and the moon dances through the woodland glades.

She encountered a guide, an animal with the spirit flame in its eyes as she wandered through the undergrowth, through nature itself. In the mystery of her being she saw a great pool of liquid. The pool that contains the un-manifested power of woman to bring all things into creation. The moon shone a shaft of light down into the dark pool spiralling her down at the speed of light on a mysterious journey to the black sun, heading towards eternity into the never ending depth of her body.

Reaching the end she met with a furnace of black compacted energy which imploded on itself. She circled it not knowing which way to enter until she was pulled into its centre, velvety and caressing. Overwhelmed she sank deeper and deeper, rolling and rotating with every atom, connected with and touched by each one.

She switched back her consciousness to the moon, the mystery of pure woman and as the moon danced on the pool of iridescent liquid, in the dark fluid ripples she could see all of life encapsulated within. All the animals appeared around her and birds flew above her, owls hooting and wolves with their fiery spiritual eyes, guiding, guarding; all coming to be joined with her as one with nature.

I saw all the spirit and psychic energies combine to create all forms of life. Everything spiritual is bonded to animal life and its flame sequence, even the animals have flames in their eyes. No mind is involved, it is the purity of the spiritual intelligence. Animals, like us are God in their pure form, but they do not oppose nature as man does, they work with it having no ego body only an earth spirit. Their earth spirit consciousness is unlimited. So they are there, in the pure mystique of woman, where the hoot of the owl becomes a beautiful song, where the wolves are there to protect and guide you instinctively deeper and deeper into your mystery; the pure female spirit, into the earth Womb within the body. Leading you to your first home with the earth spirit.

As I watched, everything came into creational form. I was caught up in its mystery and feeling and it was breathtaking. Sometimes it is too much to bear for as the sensation moves around my body, I wonder why I need return to the physical world with all its suffering and I long to remain in this place. For woman this is her reality, this is her being, this is what she longs to be united with; her Love in the nurturing of the animals; the Love the mother gives to the young; life as it is before it takes the form of the physical world. The intelligence of the earth's spirits, her natural state. She craves to manifest directly from her own body.

She was led into the animal Womb by her wolf guide, a magnificent place to be marvelled where all birth takes place. His eyes ablaze looking at her, he commanded her to be aware of everything around her. She saw that in this womb, all of creation is the spirit animals coming into physical form in a different way to the physical birth of animals in our world. She saw the animal flame, the pure essence of all life, creating them in the spiritual animal kingdom, and a shower of sparks bursting forth from the flame. Life itself splitting the flame asunder from one big flame a shower of tiny sparks

From the rabbit, to the crocodile, to the deer, each carry a little flame and all life manifests through it. It is an indescribable state and a beauty no woman should miss seeing, for she does the same in her own body. She is the giver of life everything comes from her. She spreads her beauty upon the earth for all to see and be nourished by it. This is the place where I joined with God and, by His grace, I entered into the centre of my being.

The Light Blue Flame of Animal Life

The light blue flame is the flame of animal intelligence. It is one of the most enthralling because everything happens instantaneously with animals so that the results can be directly linked to the inner experience, unlike people who allow time to obstruct their development.

I was working with two ladies who insisted on staying together throughout their sessions. Being good friends, they wanted to enter the earth Womb together to share this unique experience. It usually takes me no time at all to guide people there, but for some reason I was hampered in taking one of the ladies in. Puzzled by this, thinking that perhaps one of them was not ready for the transformation, I left it to the grace of a greater power.

Several months later the same lady rang me in a very distressed state asking to see me as soon as possible. Her much loved young dog had died. She had gone away for a weekend and had put the dog in kennels and she felt that the dog must have been mistreated there. When I looked inside her I beheld a most wonderful sight. Her lovely dog had given up its life willingly to lead her into the earth Womb and the fires. What immense integrity our animals have. I have seen this happen on other occasions since, and I know that they have the same life force as equal pure intelligence as us. They come to us, their loved ones, to aid us spiritually showing us the true value of our earth spirit.

Surrender

As I surrender myself to this power within then all things are made possible. I let go of memory for the mystery of woman is all life now, imminent life becoming form all around me. This is spiritual presence. I then became aware, returning back into my senses, back into reality and the physical world; an easy painless transition. When you look into the body with your pure mental energy, you begin to look without using your memory; it is by-passed. Love will take those women, who are endeavouring to bring spiritual Love onto the earth, into this mysterious place.

I have learned to give up thinking and put myself into the hands of the greater power. Intuition is my Love conveying the truth and I experience the truth increasingly more profoundly and more frequently. Intuition, the feeling aspect of Love, is given to you connecting you with what is intimately yours and to protect you in the physical world. My whole life has become an observation, I observe the body from inside. If you rely on being the observer of yourself and trust in your perception it will show you the beauty in the natural world that will bring you Paradise on earth, the Golden Age. As you become more accustomed to moving deeper into your solar plexus, you find the sun nucleus on the inside as well as the sun outside. The two suns in perfect union is what I know to be Paradise on earth.

Chapter xvii

The Serpent In The Corn

In the spring of 1990 I saw the first physical evidence of the great serpent that I had been seeing in vision. I was at home with a friend who researches crop circles. We had just had lunch and moved into my workroom to talk. I put a disc in the player and slipped into an altered state.

We felt the power rise in the room and a great voice spoke through me and introduced himself as Omra Kuamra Sheeana. I had never spoken in another tongue before and it was a surprise to us both. The voice announced that when the serpent appears in the corn fields human consciousness would rise on the planet, and it would take place later this year. The name was unknown to me, so I rang a Jewish man I had worked with. He did not understand it but some days later after talking to a Rabbi friend he rang to tell me it was ancient Aramaic and that it had been Christ introducing himself; Sheeana meaning Redeemer.

Later that year, whilst visiting the same friend a crop circle specialist popped in on his way home from a site visit. To our amazement, that day he had discovered a cropmark in the form of a serpent and he showed us his drawings of it. I told him of my prediction earlier that year and what it meant but he dismissed it, unaware of the true meaning of what the serpent represents.

Genuine cornfield configuration represents the spiritual purpose of those working for the planet's renewal, to end its loveless deterioration The cosmic serpent continually giving life to the earth womb where our greed has raped it's energies and resources. I continue to see many wondrous visions of the cosmic serpent's interaction with the earth. And Mother Nature responds with these wondrous displays of cosmic signs symbolic of her supremacy, proving she will not be abused or ignored. My friend and I continued to work in this area, but eventually I was drawn deeper within whilst she continued her crop circle studies.

The Temple of Law

Out on the skyline of the wide open plain the temple pillars stood tall and strong, a circle of stone with the flame of Love contained within, burning bright at the altar. It was winter with a crisp and pleasant chill in the air. Arm in arm the Revealer and the Goddess walked together towards the sacred temple.

In the magic of the moon light they stood, and She looked into His eyes. The Revealer in total surrender had come to resurrect this place of Love and law, and in cosmic alignment give all to woman in Her mystery, the Goddess in time. Revealer of the truth and the law, he called the energies down from the sky to break the old patterns and realign them through cosmic implosion.

He stood back to await the energies of the great planets, drawn down from the heavens by the cosmic vortex, to circle the sky in alignment above the flame of Love burning at the altar. With a momentous eruption the awesome cosmic energies exploded and their sacred law was encoded within the temple stones.

The Revealer explained that when I could take the force of the cosmic vortex into my body, unified with the Love I carry within, the uncontrollable energies on our planet would be neutralised. I would then live in the physical the true Goddess energy. And all women with me could similarly take in this energy, through the Love they carry, to walk into the new Paradise earth.

For when these wayward energies on our planet are purified and distilled down to the vital essence of the body energy, they can be compacted into the physical body and the permanent golden body within. Once neutralised the energies are used to create Paradise. Then we will be equipped to go through the time barrier and enter the new dimension consciously and spiritually, leaving behind the world of karmic energies, suffering and emotion. All energies for our new world must be gathered from this one and carried in our bodies.

The Revealer started to work at the altar, to draw through the flames the memory sealed in the stones in ancient language. Slowly the stones came alive and moving gracefully in rhythm to the Revealer's voice they circled around them. The upright pillars transformed into Gods, tall and stately, cloaked in fine array with their hands high, supporting the recumbent Goddess stones skywards, an offering to the cosmos aligning their Love for the universe.

Then the flames opened to reveal to her the ancient truth held within. She could see the tree of life. Each bough held a myriad of patterns of life, one pattern for each creation. And there, she could see a new bough growing with a unique pattern forming for the creation of Paradise, that woman in her Love fulfilled by man of Love would build.

The Star Of Peace

Circling the temple above, awaiting command
The Revealer and Goddess standing below, hand in hand.
Immersed in their Love they have come to heal,
Releasing us from the trap of our self made will.

Signalling above them, the star of peace,
Time has come to its end, the final conclusion.
The circle of time diminished and withered,
Consumed by the circling flame of Love,
Sacrifice on this earth will be no more.

The altar once fallen, as knowledge long lost,
Now springs forth the tree of life
With its new code for mankind.

This temple of our land has stood the test of time,
Guardian of the new pattern therein
Until the Revealer and Goddess come together in Love,
Unlocking in time the sacred law.

Universal Consciousness

A part of the sun broke into minute particles and extended towards her forming a golden thread for her to follow. Her solar body had become weightless and she flew effortlessly to where the light led her, past the brightness of the sun out into a universe populated with myriads of stars radiating ethereal silver light. As she stared spellbound at the sheer beauty of this incredible display, she was astounded to see a spaceship approach with people peering out from the portholes beckoning her towards an open doorway in the side of the ship.

About six months later I experienced this vision in externalised form. Around this time I had started to visit sacred sites around England. In vision, powerful symbols of the sun and moon would draw me to them to celebrate the solstice and equinox. On one occasion I had gone to Avebury to celebrate the summer solstice and I was sitting with a group of people on the grass in the centre of the henge, when I went into vision.

I could see light shining from a crystalline form hovering above, the same magnificent light that had led me down into the solar centre within my body. Then an awesome spaceship descended from the heavens and moved down The Avenue towards us. It was the size of the whole of Avebury covering all four fields. Coloured lights revolved beneath the craft and thousands of cosmic beings, robed so I could not see their form rather like the spirits in the earth Womb, were lowered to the ground near the central stone in the Cove. They encircled the stones and moved towards us to merge with our bodies, which took on a vibrating light energy. We accompanied them back to the central stone and were raised up into the spaceship.

The Gathering

As my consciousness expanded I experienced an increasing number of visions of spaceships, always accompanied by a feeling of deep and profound spiritual union. One day whilst meditating I was pulled through a tube of light, ascending higher and higher, with numerous spiritual people I knew journeying to the same place. A few moments later I felt an intense energy in my body as a tingling and change of consciousness and I sat down to be still.

She was swiftly drawn up a green shaft of light overlooking a vast area of the country. People, many of whom she knew, were gathering in various places. They seemed instinctively to know what they were doing and everyone was calm and orderly.

She could see over one of the gatherings a giant crystal hovering in the sky and the facets of the giant crystal opened, unfolding to reveal an enormous revolving spacecraft. The bottom of the craft dropped away and several giant stairways were lowered and the crowds beneath began to board assisted by cosmic beings.

Then she was thrust down into the crowds and turned to see her sister who handed over her seven year old daughter and said, "Look after her, I know she will be safe." She took hold of the child's hand and together they boarded the spacecraft. Then the undercarriage was raised and the spacecraft changed back into its crystal form and sped back deep into the universe.

My sister has no psychic or spiritual knowledge but she commented that at the time of my vision, which had lasted several days, her daughter had suffered an inexplicable illness and had been muttering that she was going "up and out". On the day my vision ended, she recovered.

Through these visions I understood the vastness of what was happening to humanity. Thousands of people are being prepared for universal consciousness as we come face to face with ourselves in the cosmos at the beginning of time, thereby closing the cycle of time. Many people will experience a loss of time as they frantically try to hold on to each time frame in their life. They are rushing around trying to take on too many tasks, to complete that which can never be completed, grasping at empty experiences that will not enhance their life, becoming exhausted before final release. But as I also realised, my vision of universal consciousness is of no use unless it is grounded in some way on a practical level, brought into the physical world to make it a reality in their everyday life. To take the ultimate step of making the intellectualised image a physical reality on this earth.

Meeting New People
More and more spiritual people were coming into my life; 'spiritual' meaning awakening to the knowledge we are all one and God is not separate from you in any instance. As I received more Love a deep feeling of peace and stillness came over me, which I felt particularly with this group of healers, spiritual students and teachers and sacred site travellers as I

worked with them. They had accumulated the energy of these places in their bodies and I could sense a great exchange between us during the times we were together. I remember it was a wonderful summer.

This was the beautiful beginning of my relationship with these people and my visions of union with cosmic beings, symbolic of universal consciousness. I explained to them what I was seeing, that I realised my consciousness was opening up and I was moving into a new enlightened state, a new energy of harmony and balance; cosmos and earth in union. The powerful feeling of universal impersonal Love which I could feel as a warmth in my body flowing from head to toe, so overwhelming at times I would go into what appeared like a deep sleep not being able to move or speak.

As demonstrated by these experiences, my mental energy was changing but it was by no means cleansed completely. We have to root ourselves back into our bodies more and more deeply for the final cleansing. Balance and cleansing is vital to bring love into the world, mental purification expanding cosmically. Spirituality is the nucleus of love in a body. The void is then accessed through the stillness of love. This is a process that never ends.

Chapter xviii

The Well of Blood

I was in two worlds at once. My consciousness had split and I was being shown remarkable things that were working out in the material world. I knew spirituality has to have tangible results to be the truth and I was experiencing actual physical healing. One evening my husband and I were listening to some music. I was swept away with its ambience. The blue flame rose in front of me, as if gathering from the sound all around the room. It was enchanting as it engaged my attention, then divided into three.

The blue flames emanating from the blue pillar were fascinating. Everything could be manifested from them. As she watched, three blue flames dancing before her came together and changed into angels and then into the cowled forms, the presence of the spirit cloaked so she could see them. She had seen the angels and the cowled forms before and today through the flames, the earth Womb unfolded like a beautiful picture book, the pages coming alive in front of her. It was magical.

She could hear lovely music and a soft warm feeling rising in her body. The three cowled forms came together as one flame and as she descended into her body she was drawn closer and closer to a well-like structure, with the powerful feeling in her body that there was something within that was demanding recognition. She summoned her courage to peep over the top.
It was full of blood. An intense feeling rose in her to go through the blood. As the pull became stronger she lowered herself in. To her surprise, rising from the centre she could see

a beautiful clear, mirror-like flame dancing around her in acknowledgement caressing her spiritual body. She was joined with the flame and descended down into the well of sacred blood, the purified sacred blood of all women that runs through the universal Womb.

As she descended, the sacred blood and the flame became one. Instinctively she knew she could trust in this power she was entering. The mirror like flame reflected the presence of other women in the blood, women she did not know, who she was to meet later in life

I heard the lovely music again. I was back again in my world; the two worlds came together. I could feel the well of blood rise in my body and I felt safe in the warmth of the love and the feeling of compassion. Then I felt the cold spiritual fire in my eyes they were like ice. I opened my eyes to see three tears on my cheek, teardrops of blood, three large drops, the same number as the flames, had dropped onto my dress. They were tears of sacred blood purifying my body to let the cosmic Love to pour in. Love and spirit joined with the physical world, heaven and earth, union in perfect balance.

I began to see images of Christ on the cross reflected in the men around me. His body was an olive colour and his hair was jet black. He always seemed to be a little unkempt but with a rugged face of deep understanding, as if he knew what I was going through. I realised that the crucifixion symbolises killing off the lower self to make way for the consciousness of Love.

My mind tried to rationalise these experiences but it was lost. To take responsibility for this spiritual life I had to know what I was doing and how I was going to bring this Love and beauty into the physical world permanently.

The Vicar

I had read about our vicar who was featured in our local paper for his good works in the community. I thought it would be a good place to start so I went to see him on his afternoon surgery. After being shown in, sitting opposite him, I explained my vision and the Love I felt. He looked surprised and said he could not help me and that perhaps I was going mad. I felt let down by this man who represented God and left.

I experienced these and other Christian images of religious suffering, instilled into me when I was young. As I made them conscious they transformed back to formless Love and things began to change in my life. The Revealer, stepping in where man had failed, came to me to take my distress away. He told me I was to move beyond man's law. I was to be joined to my eternal male, in the presence of God.

Chapter xix

The Twin Flame

She found herself face to face with a burning silver cross and behind it a vast vibrating energy. Its magnetic power pulled her forward, creating a deep feeling of peace in her body. From behind the energy, two blue flames of the divine will moved out to stand at the right arm and another at the left arm of the cross. As she looked in amazement she felt within a deep knowledge that something powerful was happening to her.

When the recognition was complete within her body, the cross began to spin. The two blue flames were drawn in unison towards the centre of the cross and down the shaft spinning and spiralling at a tremendous speed. Then the flaming cross sank down into the earth. She sensed in her body a feeling of gently rising and then falling into a beautiful sense of completeness.

The Ring of Fire

The Revealer came to her and told her to prepare herself for God. She instantly felt a rush of energy pour into her ears and she went with it, her spirit moving at a tremendous pace along what seemed like a long wide shaft of white, silver and blue light. She gradually became aware of the tunnel of light opening out into a vast expanse of timeless space, into which she dropped, with an encircling bowl of blue life-giving energy that cushioned her fall. She realised she had stopped moving and all was perfectly still. She was in the void.

As she waited in anticipation she felt an intelligence move into the energy field; colours formed and then burst into brightly coloured flames. She was not afraid and felt only a deep peace and an acute awareness of what was taking place. She heard a gentle but strong voice call her name from a long way off, calling louder and louder until it seemed to surround her.

She was in a situation of no time, no gravity and no direction with only the voice all around her. Then an intense beam of light with immense life-giving properties focused on her and burst into a circle of flames. Standing by her side the Revealer reassured her that all was well. The flames began to expand and as she looked, she could see within them an incredible depth that appeared to go on forever. She felt the Revealer draw her attention back to keep her conscious for she was becoming absorbed by the energy before her.

And she heard the voice again and it said, " The Revealer has guided you here so you may enter the circle of fire at the centre of the cross. You cannot see me for I am everything in creation, I am omnipotent and if you step over the time barrier into me, your creator, you will have the complete and absolute union you desire, with the divine energy of Love.

"There are no conditions, you have left time and existence behind you and I direct your life in all its ways. You will never know what I will call on you to do, but if you give up your will, you will receive all knowledge of life on this earth and in the cosmos and the reason for humanity and your purpose as part of it. I am the only power in the universe able to keep your body alive after death in this life. I will take you through death consciously and show you how to keep the body pure. Entering the Ring of Fire you will secure a new line of destiny, by dying into the opposite, and I will close the circle of time."

I wanted to ask questions of what had been said but there was no time. As I turned to look at the Revealer for assurance, the circle of flames sprang up around me and I felt within me a deep feeling of magnetic union which drew me deep towards the flames. I was choiceless; the power was too great. I was about to discover the mystery of God.

As she moved deep into the circle of flames she was suspended in space, floating with a whirling of energies around her, caressing her spirit body; immersed in the moment, trusting in the Love of the divine that had sustained her in so many ways. As she looked into the expanse she saw the world floating and pulsating, turning gracefully with a web of brightly coloured lines moving through it, flashing with sparks of energy where one line interconnected with another. The crossover points of the earth and the cosmic energies held in timeless presence by the circle of flames.

She was drawn to one crossover point in particular to connect with the flashing orb of energy at the centre. The voice spoke again, " The crossover point you are drawn to is your chosen destiny to follow the law of God which releases you from fate, the law of man. You will carry the energy of it back to earth in your body until the time of death and on through to eternity. Many enter the crossover point throughout their lives only to leave disappointed. But sufficient energy has been gathered by you to collect and flood in at the crossover point enabling you to make the connection".

The power of the energies became too intense for me to bear and I lost all sense of awareness. My next realisation was that I had returned to my physical body. Several hours had elapsed but the Revealer was still with me and He gently assured me that my entry into the mystery of God was not a dream. He explained that those who enter the circle of fire, the centre of all life where only purity resides, unite with that which created them. And they suffer no more on the earth, guided by the power of life that knows no end to do life's bidding. This is the great and mysterious journey into God.

110

Cosmíc MasteR

I had no idea of the true significance of this experience or others that I had seen. A friend suggested I went to see a Polish cosmic master whom she had recently heard giving a talk at a Mind, Body and Spirit meeting in London. I arranged to see him on my way up to a concert at the Royal Albert Hall. He was warm and friendly and after making me comfortable through his interpreter he asked me the reason for my visit. I told him of my visions.

In response he spoke to me at length on the significance of Love and universal consciousness. Firstly, he made reference to the universal symbol of the monad. The circle at the centre of the cross symbolises God consciousness. The vertical shaft leading down from it represents the flow of energy from heaven to earth. The right arm of the cross is the energy of God coming into creation and the left arm the soul. The soul touches both the inner realm of the spirit, from which it receives direct inspiration, and the external world from which it receives impressions. The whole symbolises the divine principle that gives life and consciousness to all form; the creational ray from the universal absolute principle; the ultimate atom. He explained that universal consciousness could only be achieved through man and woman entering the circle together in union and that a man would come to me and I would know him. He would seek me out and take me into the universal consciousness.

We would then join with twelve other couples with the same universal consciousness to form a new body, and that in the next few years space craft would be landing on earth to take couples on board in groups of twelve. I would be one of the first few hundred to leave the planet, with thousands of others joining us later. I asked if I would be with my husband and he said that cannot be a personal decision, for the universe chooses with whom we go.

He explained my vision of the burning cross represents eternal divine Love, which manifests on this earth extremely rarely. The eternal Love between the divine principle of man and woman, which rarely happens before death and was of great significance in my life. The vision signified that the male principle, which has been within me forever, was about to manifest for me on the earth.

He said all my fears about Love and life would be alleviated and that year I would find the man who was to take me to cosmic consciousness. I asked if I was to be with this man forever and he said that the man has always been with me. I was in a daze at what had been said. I thanked him for his knowledge and Love and left.

A New Creation

This experience seemed to link with a vision I had seen earlier that year whilst sitting in the garden, that communicated the same knowledge on a more earthly level.

In among the bushes she saw a huge toad that led her into the earth Womb. She could see a whole universe and it was beautiful, a matrix of floating gentle colours and she floated with them. Then she perceived a single point of powerful energy, a tiny universe in its entirety, an egg suspended in the cavity of the earth Womb. Billions of sperm were frantically trying to puncture and fertilise the egg in their intense desire for life. Then one sperm finally succeeded in piercing through the egg wall, which like an infinitely tiny atom exploded into life.

The intensity suddenly ceased and all the other sperm dropped away. In their millions the sperm had been instinctively acting as a support system to the one successful sperm, as the workers support the queen bee, helping to build an intense energy, a point of power that implodes to bring about the moment of creativity. She realised she was observing the fertilisation of the earth Womb, this she understood was to create pure spiritual and physical impersonal Love. The infinitesimal point of the creative universal will where the point becomes the whole, everything and nothing. The power of stillness combined with absolute awareness of the whole of creation.

Chapter xx

The White and Gold Cosmic Flame

The white and gold cosmic flame contains conjoined within it the silvery-white lunar flame of the moon, the female principle and the gold solar flame of the sun, the male principle. The blazing gold of the solar male inside every man is his power to activate the solar atom in the female solar centre, during love making it is felt as warmth, and bliss in their bodies. It ensures that the Love purifies them of accumulated past and helps to keep them free of suffering.

The lunar female Love for cosmic male grounded on this earth as physical Love is experienced in the pure feeling body as a sublime liquid intelligence, the essential presence of all life that moves vibrantly around the body releasing immense joy to the lovers. It is the female protecting the male, the female energy that has always protected the male in the microcosm and nourished him in the physical world through the creation. It is the purity of this precious feeling that joins, protects and keeps vigil over the opposite. The source of all life arises from these two principles.

As she drew nearer something spoke to her through her being. She could see encircling and swirling around the flame a blazing, liquid energy. The angels led her into the white and gold liquid fire. It ran through her body like quicksilver and she eagerly moved towards the centre of the flame, drawn like a moth to the light, mesmerised by the power of its beauty. She felt that her body would burn up and when she could go no closer, the angels came out of the flame and transported her into its heart. Within the core of the flame, in this single infinitesimal point, all the atoms that had ever been in man on this earth were now contained.

The energy burned and swept around her, a raging beautiful fire caressing her very soul. This same soul had struggled for so long, almost to the point of death, to reach this truth within. She could feel the flame blazing through her body, consuming the mental and physical pain, and transforming it into the flame's own purity. She moved deeper and deeper within, aware that she was being cleansed to the depths of her physical soul.

Thus cleansed she was within reach of the golden cosmic male energy and a magnificent explosion took place inside her. Her whole body began to oscillate in acknowledgement of the vibration of universal spiritual life. Joy sang out and she felt cleansed and renewed. She stayed there; it seemed like forever, suspended in this timeless place.

When she was released from the flame she could see encircled around the fire several beautiful cowled forms. She instantly recognised them as the spirits who had given her healing earlier in her life and she was taken to be joined with them as one in impersonal spiritual Love.

My New Awareness

I was becoming quite at home with the new spiritual awareness but there seemed to be no one around who could help me further with it. This did not worry me to much because with the feeling of the infinite Love of the earth Womb all my fears were washed away. I would return there every day and experience the union I needed. As I became more accustomed to the reality of what was going on within and around me I realised that I needed to go there more often and I was willing to give up anything to return to this place of harmony and balance.

The Sun Body

Following my visit to the Polish cosmic master, I started to see a featureless golden body representing the union of cosmos and earth, sun and nature, male and female spiritual bodies combined. I had seen this shadowing the cosmic master moving within and outside his body and I could see these golden bodies of solar consciousness are identical to the physical body. They are permanent, giving us the right energy to move into the spiritual realms to build our world of Love in the paradise earth.

I had felt my own golden body yielding to his with a yearning to move out from the matter of my own body and a tearing sensation inside my physical body, as the cosmic golden body attempted to step outside of it.   And all this accompanied by a feeling of deep and intense Love. As I went deeper into the vision of golden bodies I could see a number of them interacting with my own body and with nature. I knew that somehow my physical body needed to become sufficiently soft and malleable for it to step out.

Presence

Flickering deep within our being,
The flame of Love, our perfect being.
Our union that we seek in life;
The gift, the grace, our link with God.
Unfurling, yielding, imploring your attention,
Patient, giving, never demanding.

God's world opening, announcing its presence,
Mystery awaits the journey into Love.
Captures, enraptures in it's embrace,

Holding, enfolding your spirit being.
The spirit body, returned to Love
Your union with the point of God.

To meet beyond the realms of this world,
Held in suspension, between time.
God draws you back with Love's pure grace,
To acquiesce within your sacred space.
The flame that flickers never dies
In truth and Love, God's presence held.

Chapter xxi

The Breath of Life

After this, I felt my life take a new turn. I was experiencing the two worlds of spiritual Love and the pure psychic mind more and more in vision, as they come together. I had a deep yearning for the union I had witnessed in my vision earlier in the year of the burning cross to manifest in form.

She was commanded to prepare herself for the breath of life. As these words were uttered in her body she was transported into a magnificent garden. The birds were singing and a stream was gently trickling. There was an indescribable stillness and sweetness in the air and a powerful feeling of rightness and mastery. Her conscious awareness hovered over the garden waiting for something to happen.

Then she saw the earth move and a splendid russet coloured man rose up from beneath it and sat brushing the soil from his body. He stood up and she saw he had a glowing sun for his face. He began to walk across the earth as though looking for something. She saw a speck of light, pure intelligence, emanate from his body to dance ahead and he began to follow it; through the garden, past the trees and flowers heading towards a large tree.

Instinctively now, he knew where to look. He knelt down at the foot of the tree and began to scrape away the soil uncovering a female form beneath the earth. He brushed away the soil from the contours of her body, smoothed her face clean, pulled her up out of the earth and gently laid her on the ground to look at her. She shimmered like wax, beautiful, soft and yielding. He

*tried to bring her to life, caressing and stroking her face to
wake her up.*

*Then he raised her up to him and blew the breath of life into
her and she awakened to his gentle and tender touch. In that
moment they looked at each other in wonder and awe
transfixed by their timeless Love for one another. She had
reached her earth spirit; they were together, now she was free.*

*She looked around her in amazement, absorbing the
magnificent sights of the life to which she had been born.
Everything in the garden was held in timeless beauty with a
vibrancy of colour and pristine beauty unknown in our world.
Nothing diminished or decayed. Adam, her man, brought her
fruits to eat, serving her devotedly and she began to grow
strong. He sat her up against the trunk of the tree to bathe her
with water from the stream.*

*Everything that passed between them was devotion from him.
He served her ceaselessly; she only had to breathe and he was
there for her, giving her all she needed. Indeed he was her sole
source of life, for without his Love, attention and devotion she
would expire. His unique care for her being the natural
expression of man born of woman's earth womb in the first
creation. Both pure spiritual forms are still there in the garden
of Love, bringing alive in you that which is rightfully yours,
your eternal love the earth spirit. This can only be realised and
entered through Love.*

The Psychic Web

In all women is the deep and profound knowledge of the
mystery of the earth.   This is the primal instinctive mystery
of woman, her wholeness that links her to God's creation; all
form in the physical universe; all manifested Love on the
earth. This is her true identity.

In her search to unite with what she knows to be her true nature, (her earth spirit with earthman that she embodied at the beginning of time) she enters the inner world within her body, the vastness of the psychic web of all life. As she crosses the great divide between the tangible outer physical world and the intangible inner pure psychic world, she meets the mass of formless matter from the unformed, streaming towards her with unrelenting speed out into this world. And confusion begins as she gets caught up in it, not knowing which way to go, to go on through it or come back into the physical world.

Deep below this teeming mass through which she struggles to cross, is the pure unchanging, undeniable quality of her creational mystery. The dark pool of unformed life in woman's Womb, the primal energy, and the purity, which we see manifested in this earth as all of God's creation through her.

She enters the river of her pure feeling, the liquid substance that runs through all life. She knows it only through instinct, but trusting in her connection to it through her Love of her outer creation, she desperately tries to reach it on the inside, to unite with earthman to keep the spark of all life alive.

This pure feeling carries her deeper into the depths of her body psyche bringing her in contact with the inner world on a mystery journey of no end, eventually to flood and fill her being with this life-giving substance. She will have many unforgettable earthly experiences to accompany it, sometimes undergoing great suffering, to bridge the gap to reach and sustain this power that she knows she is, to keep her creation in nature alive.

She has to let go of the physical world and trust in the power of pure feeling. But the unrelenting passion that bubbles in the place of union builds up in her with immense pressure as she nears her destination, causing her great distress as she struggles to unify the inner beauty with the outer creation. Becoming too powerful to bear, her searching yields no reward. Unable to find her correct mirror in life to propel her forward into the spirit of Love, she halts perplexed with nowhere to go.

In exhausted desperation she ceases all trying, all effort is released and in her desolation she walks into the barren wilderness of hopelessness within. In her distress and confusion blind panic sets in. She runs into the world for help, often not finding it and she can lose all touch with the pure feeling within her. Nothing then can bridge the gap and she feels lost, let down and deserted, often not knowing why. Man can love her back to her earth spirit allowing the destructive ego consciousness to die naturally. In this transformation woman uses her wisdom and integrity and man keeps her alive by his love for her.

Her intuitive knowledge of the truth, which runs so deep within, can draw to her a life experience to connect her to the power. Only when she is alert enough to realise the truth of conscious experience, to live her feeling as pure movement with action in life, can the two worlds be in balance. Her experience is unconscious when woman grasps at anything offered her in the world, in the vain hope that the world can fill her unrelenting desire to unite with the essence of her being. Unless offered in Love these experiences are empty and the flow of life is stagnant and oppressed. Conscious experience through the creative experiences of the natural world, of right lovemaking and good childbirth in a loving partnership can often link her back to her pure feeling through web of life.

Woman today living a loveless life is an empty reflected body in time, wandering the earth and the inner wilderness of her being, crying. Unknowing why emptiness invades the vastness of her inner world, leaving her to the mercy of her mind, whilst she searches for the inner Goddess of all life to fill her and lead her to her rightful place.

By connecting to your spiritual twin, you will be led through the mysterious realms of all the other worlds to where the Goddess resides, the inner sacred chambers, the point of creation, in your Womb. When the time is right you will be filled with the life-giving substance of your true essence pouring into your body ensuring you attract men of Love. Where there is no man in your life the Goddess with her protective veil prepares you for your journey into Love.

When woman's true nature unfolds through right experience in life she connects with the pure feeling and feels within her a movement of life, a union, a connection she has not felt before. She knows something profound has taken place for which there is no explanation in this world. This is the mystery and power of woman in balance with the rhythm of nature.

As the feeling takes her deeper, she floats towards an incomprehensible power. She feels the pressure build up in her again, the struggle to find a way to bring her experience of this unknown power into her life, to hold the inner and outer worlds in balance. When the Love and beauty entering her mind become too much too powerful to bear she sinks into the pure feeling of Love and her passage then becomes easier. She is now flowing in this great river of pure feeling, into the power of her own creation with the God energy, the pure flame of Love and the living waters of all life.

She knows that meeting this pure flame of Love of all creation behind time has brought her to the two most powerful elements in the universe. The opposite principle of pure man, pure woman. They blend together and the feeling is ecstatic; union has taken place. They have found each other behind space and time, each instinctively knowing the power and place of the other. The unrelenting universal law of Love that forever draws you nearer to the sacred land within, to join in rhythmic and harmonious union with your divine opposite, in the twin flames, held by the stillness in the presence of God.

Through the passion and Love of the opposites in union, the flame of passion and the feeling waters of life, the flow of the creation of all life back out into the earth is replenished; man and woman then know their natural state of divine being.

Man - The Hunter And Lover

Deep within every man is the ever present knowledge of his place in the natural kingdom. He is the hunter and the lover, replenishing his energy through the hunt to serve his woman, the Goddess energy, so that she may nourish the creation. Only through serving woman and the creation can the full potential of man be realised.

In the sacred land of the spirit, where all life is one, God man walks the forest. His animal guide, the wolf, with the blaze of the spirit in his eyes, lights his way to the place where small animals lie in the undergrowth and he gathers them up into his pouch of woven willow. These are the animals that have died to give their life force to God man, for him to give the eternal life-giving energy to energise the Goddess Womb.

The Hunter

Looking into each others eyes,
They know the vow made long ago:
To keep the cycle of creation anew,
The hunt to replenish all will ensue.

The stag runs ahead out of sight,
God man follows, the hunt is right.
His weapon, of pure psychic vision,

He enrobes his body in nature's power.
Animal and man unified as one.

He feels the vibration intensify
As the stag evades him all the way,
He pursues the stag to the end of the chase.
They regard each other face to face.

Bare hands upon antlers, God man holds
This noble creature for as long as he can,
Until all the energy from the stag
Pours forth into man; this is the divine plan.

The struggle is long, each knowing no release
Until God man brings the majestic animal down.
To master the animal is the strength he needs
To Love the Goddess to continue the law,
Keeping the cycles of nature forever pure.

On the waves of her power,
Through the dome of her Womb
The noble animal stirs

When God man has depleted his animal stock in the hunting ground, he enters the sacred ground of the Goddess, a power dome, where all life is abundant, formed from the radiance of her divine Womb. A rainbow dome, a great sea of undulating waves of colour emanating from her, it extends out into the forest to replenish the forest of his hunting grounds.

And he awaits her there, for in his absence she is visiting her temple to drink of the life-giving nectar that flows there to sustain her, connecting her directly to God. The distilled essence of all life formed from all creations that the Godhead stores and keeps. Through her divine link to man, the Goddess picks up his vibration; in her radiance she enters the dome and the birds sing her praise. She goes towards him to her sacred throne where he has laid out the animals gathered for her on the earth.

With a flash of energy from her body, she regenerates them, directly injecting them with her being. They come back to life, to move and scurry away back into the forest. These are the blue prints of the creation forever in her Womb and mind. Keeping her mind pure and regenerated, linking her to all life.

Eternal Bliss

In front of the fire of eternal bliss
The goddess sits singing her song
Of God man's devotional Love.

An ode to God for the Love and peace,
For the devotion and power she knows.
How to contain this Love forever pure
In her creational Womb is unknown.

In his Love of her, sensing her presence
God man enters the sacred ground
Unable to stay away a moment too long.
In a flash of intense recognition
She senses his footsteps and his echo of her song,
As he is drawn towards her in the sacred ground.

The spirit fire now rages in ecstatic delight,
The earth pulse begins, the time is now right.
Given to each other, a gift from the divine,
Only God in creation knows when lovers unite.

This Love, a union of purity, a God given idea,
To blend together in exquisite delight.
The intensity binds them in pleasure and bliss
The protected Love that knows no blight.

The protecting fire sheds impurities away,
The sacred veil hides all from human eyes.
This is not God's disguise.

This is divinity from the depths of our being
Bringing all lovers back to the beginning;
To where Love resides deep in our heart
To keep our dignity at the centre, the spark
Where God's knowledge for lovers reside,
That can only be seen in each other's eyes.

Love that remains forever-undivided in time,
Love that never fails us, the union divine.
Man and woman creating with the passion of God,
The divine Womb of woman and her Godly man.

From the eternal fire of bliss their Love bursts forth,
Rapturous in its desire, compelling the lovers to express all
From the point of creation within
Her only desire, to express her Love to man and all creation
Delivering into time the divine laws,

Each touching the spark, to protect the creation.
Entwined forever in their beloved hearts,
The Love that is made through the nature of God
This power will sustain us, by God's command.

Chapter xxii

Master of Love

At this time in my life I was feeling somewhat desperate. I was being shown such vast contrasts of experience in the mental and spiritual field. Such was my confusion that I was not sure which world I was in. It was all becoming too much and I was finding it increasingly difficult to hold on to my physical body, which felt like it was breaking up. I needed something to bring it all together though I did not know what. In my job as a professional counsellor I knew I must seek help of a practical nature so I consulted with one of my colleagues.

An elderly lady fifteen years my senior, Sandra was not surprised when I told her of my experiences. We talked for a while and it became evident she had a similar understanding as myself. She told me she had recently been to see an Australian spiritual master, Barry Long and suggested that I might like to accompany her on his next seminar in England. I wondered about Barry Long and if he could be of help. There was so much to say and tell him it could not be contained within a letter so I plucked up the courage to put it on tape and sent it to him.

Two weeks later I received a lengthy letter from Barry Long and he seemed to answer most of my questions and put at ease my fears of going mad. He explained my fear was the response of my analytical, mental process of the brain whereas all the visions and intuitions I had described were perceptions of the deep spiritual psyche. He went on to say the scientific brain is purely a phenomenon of the psyche, an instrument for making and handling material connections, whilst we have other means of perceiving the creative symbols of the psyche that vary according to the spiritual intelligence of the individual.

He recommended that I keep imagination out of my vision and intuition for pure psychic energy only embodies that, which is without mental connections and deductions. It is pure thought free from all sense. I was very relieved to have this explained to me and to understand that my visions of beauty, Love and the universe were the truth, and that my distress was caused by my mind's interpretation of the experience, which is beyond its grasp. I realised that this was what the Revealer was trying to impart to me through my visions of Love.

Barry explained that in my vision of Adam and Eve and the fiery cross, that I, woman, was Eve. That there is only one Eve, one female principle, and millions of women are endeavouring to embody her. My vision of the conjunction of the two energies on the cross symbolises my own female principle and the male principle which can only be re-united in the inner psyche after death, or for a very few in physical existence. He also said that the outer conjunction of the two energies also occurs in the body psyche but manifests in the physical body of the opposite principle. He said that whilst this was a great rarity on this earth, it had happened to me. As within so without.

Barry explained that in his understanding both principles were too powerful to be contained within one single body and that it can only be known in the making of Love in the flesh, in union with God, making two bodies one. He said that he was always with me in the blue flame and that if I came to one of his meetings, to make myself known to him. Barry Long's next course was on cosmic consciousness at Bristol University and I booked to go.

The Course

I asked to talk to Barry if he had time. I spoke to one of the staff who later took me to him. I was very nervous at first but after a few minutes sitting in front of him, I became calm and he continued to speak to me. I told him about the vision I had experienced earlier in the week. I had seen the cosmic energies, the sun and moon in union; the sun emitting a powerful cosmic energy which surrounded the moon and then entered her. And then the sun and moon beginning their dance of all life through the matrix of the universe within my body.

He then told me to look into his eyes for as long as I could. And I remember we remained like that for some time. A powerful energy went through my body and I became cold and shivering, but I felt calm and at peace. Afterwards I returned to the meeting and delighted in the teachings, which were a confirmation of what I had been experiencing.

That night, after supper, I retired to my room but could not sleep. I was lying in bed reading when I sensed a powerful pervasive presence in the room. I became very still and then I experienced intensely deep feelings of Love in my body, which circled my body from my Womb up to my head. I instantly went into a deep state of tranquillity and then to sleep. In the morning Barry called me in to see him and asked me how I had been the previous night. I told about the powerful energy and tranquillity I had felt; he did not seemed surprised. We spoke for a while and then I went back to the meeting. I came away feeling more at ease than I had for a long time.

Chapter xxiii

New Life Forms

The day I left the meeting my husband and I went on holiday together without the children for the first time in 25 years. We had always had wonderful family holidays but it was good to explore on our own and it gave me time to absorb fully what I had experienced at Barry's meeting. Lying on the beach one day, soaking up the sun and enjoying the peace, I felt myself being lifted up a shaft of green light at a tremendous speed up to the opening to another dimension.

There she was met by cosmic forms who escorted her into the heart of a spacecraft where there were gathered more cosmic forms. They carried the flame of spiritual Love in their eyes so she felt no fear and she realised they were the embodiment of cosmic intelligence and the spirit.

I could see their bodies were similar to our own, and that they are our projected life form in another dimension where we are united with the spirit where our minds and bodies are pure enough to be at one with the whole of creation without past. They were showing me more truths of cosmic reality.

She was taken to a plinth, on which stood a large crystal protected by an energy field, which evaporated before her eyes. Within the crystal was an immense movement of green wax-like energy and the same shaft of light through which she had been transported shone upwards through the crystal and around it. She was ushered into the green shaft of light and encased in its energy. It ran up and down her body, vibrating in her, the pure fluid feeling energy of woman and her power to create. She felt it go up into her head for a short time where it seemed to explode into millions of flashes of mental images, each the beginning of a new creation. Rather like billions of flowers opening at one point in time, but contained within a microscopic point in her brain; a very powerful sensation.

She was released from the energy to find she had a new awareness, a new understanding of life and creation. She was shown around the craft which was divided into different sections each of which housed new life forms coming into being, nurtured by the cosmic beings. She looked in wonderment and felt a kinship with the new life forms, which were communicating with her and the green wax-like energy inside her body moved in acknowledgement. Behind each section of new life-forms, the craft dropped away to show her new worlds, each different, but all just as interesting and fascinating as each other. It was a beautiful and amazing dimension.

She was then led to a section of the craft filled with numerous capsules energised by coloured tubes of light energy moving through them. She felt recognition and knowing coming over her. As she walked between the capsules she saw in them people she knew on earth with the same energy of various colours and shapes passing through them. Unlike the new life forms they seemed to be in a deep unconscious state. Some were wearing head protection and they were all being monitored. She was informed these people were being revived to new life and that all the new life forms she had seen earlier were their potential new bodies. Whichever life form they drew towards them would dictate their new dimension in the cosmos.

I was being shown that all life is continuous, that we all build our new body while in the earthly one. Our new creation is opened up to each of us through our acknowledgement of the truth of creation. Love, creation and all its natural abundance must be honoured consciously in the body or you will remain in the intellectual dream of life and death instead of taking part in the regeneration of all life now.

In the green shaft I was encapsulated in pure mental energy and pure spiritual fluid feeling. I felt the balance between the two energies was right but I knew I had to bring them closer together. I was brought back to the beach down the green shaft of light. At first my body had no legs, then miraculously they reformed before my eyes and a few moments later the green shaft lifted and I was fully grounded again.

Chapter xxiv

Purified Energies

I had not seen my father for 23 years. There were things between us that were not right so we had parted. Before he died, he contacted me and I went to see him. He was dying of cancer and I was truly shocked when I saw him.

I could see in him the beautiful state of Love he had reached, which went beyond all the suffering of my early days with him. I moved into a feeling of deep and powerful Love and told him that everything was all right between us and I forgave him everything. These were the words he wanted to hear, not that I have the power to forgive anybody. He said he knew I was going with him in death, but I explained I had already overcome death and that I would take him there now consciously if he wished. He declined saying he would find out soon enough. What I did not realise was that his passing away was to lead me to experience my own physical death a couple of months later. One week later he died and I was glad I had been able to make my peace with him.

I went to see him with my sister in the chapel of repose to pay my last respects. As I was shown in I felt an unusual stillness. I moved forward to touch him and held his hand and smoothed his face, saying my goodbyes and that I would see him in the earth Womb. This was the first time in my life that I was able to talk to him and just feel pure Love. I looked towards his solar plexus and could see there the blue flame about two inches in height burning powerfully, and contained within it the vital essence of his body and the life just lived.

The funeral was a quiet affair, a small gathering of friends and family, of those closest to him including four daughters and a son. During the ceremony swirling above his coffin I could see three energy vortices. The one at his head was white, the one in the centre was the blue flame and the one at his feet was a black vortex.

The white vortex detached first and danced over to her youngest sister who had loved and nursed him. It burst into sparkling stars in acknowledgement of the Love they shared and entered the top of her head. The next energy to detach was the blue flame, which moved with blazing intensity into her solar plexus. She felt a sense of completeness with her father without any separation. The last energy, the black energy moved with precision and intelligence looking for someone to enter. It moved up and down the crematorium several times too finally find and enter her other sister.

I was shocked at what I was being shown, but I understood. The glorious white vortex links my younger sister to universal life and brings her into deep contact with the pure psychic world we see as nature. The blue flame that entered my solar plexus enhances my life by bringing me eternal Love through all life. The black vortex is the emotional suffering that enters people's bodies for reincarnation, a task that can be traumatic for the receiver.

My older sister now has the task of making this energy conscious. Sometimes this is never completed within the lifetime. And it does not stop there; it can move through generations to reappear in some unsuspecting person as an entity or possession. It some cases it permeates a new life form, the body, taking over the mind so that the person never really knows who they are. It is attracted and brought into your life by the circumstances around you; drawn through into your mind like the negative to a photograph.

Thus I was shown how the energies from a dead body divide. This is the impersonal nature of Love showing the truth of life. In our times now, with our spiritual knowledge we can stop this happening. We have the chance to purify the earth and ourselves to stop the terrible reincarnation of this black emotional energy from moving into our children. What better gift of Love can we leave our children and the earth by making our emotional energy conscious whilst still in our body. This is true spiritual Love.

The Ante Room

Two weeks later after the funeral I was taking a short rest when I felt a deep sense of peace and my father around me.

She was taken again into the earth Womb where she could see an anteroom, like a preparation room and on a stone slab her father lying with a shroud over him. He was surrounded by four cowled forms who blew the spirit into his eyes and his solar plexus. He rose from his place of rest and she went to him and led him, walking arm in arm, into the centre of the earth Womb.

The cowled forms stepped back to allow him to go wherever he willed and he moved forward to join with the many billions of pure spirits, contained there within the earth Womb. And as one the spirits rose in exultation, lifting up his body and he was reunited with them all.

And so my father showed me how to accompany him beyond death, beyond the personal self and into the Womb of all life; a great honour. For there is no separation, and there should be none on this physical earth, not through personality, status, intellect, grief or emotion. I realised that there had always been this impersonal Love between us before the mind separated us. Only when you can see with compassion that we are all one can you experience Love impersonally. And

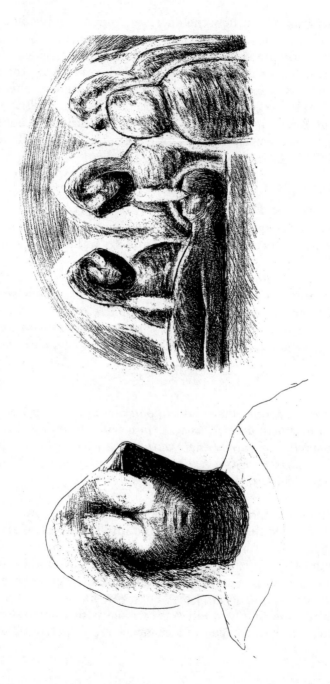

through the compassion and Love comes self-knowledge and I was determined thereafter never to allow personality to get in the way of my loving anybody ever again.

The Disguise

To make right with everybody on the earth, no matter what ills and disillusionment befall you, look behind the disguise the person wears. Behind it you only need know there is no separation and you can not allow it to happen under any circumstances whatsoever. The earth Womb of harmony and balance is a testament to universal Love; it gives to a person the Love they have not received in the world. And this energy for all humanity is within; we only need to know how to access it. To make this truth a living reality, our physical life must be right or the connection on all levels will be lost.

The Revealer appeared beside me again in the blue pillar waiting for me to link with His energies enabling me to hear His voice as an echo through my being. He explained how He had shown me the Love that all people are behind the mask of the personality and He said that it was time for me through that Love to link with all people behind time. I was not to be alarmed, for my body would go through the time barrier and be in a state of suspension in time for several weeks. I felt fearful but was instantly cleansed of all fear as the Love swept through me. The Revealer stepped back and the blue pillar reduced down to a tiny flame and was retracted back into my body.

Chapter xxv

The Embodiment

I learned that Barry Long was a tantric master, someone who can bring a person to spiritual consciousness through physical Love. I wondered how my meeting with him would affect me. A few months later my life took a turn as I went through another major experience of great impact on my life: the embodiment of the two opposite principles.

My father's funeral several months earlier had brought many questions to my mind about death. I wrote to Barry again and within a month I received a lengthy reply describing the decaying energies I was seeing in the sensory universe as the black vortex and the fluid state of the energy inside the body of matter. My experience of my father's death and Barry's letter in reply mirrored the truth of it to me and propelled me into a profound experience teaching me the purpose of death. That through death, which is Love, the creative passion is brought into the world.

One lovely May day the sight of the blossoming flowers and trees was so inviting my husband and I went out to lunch and decided on the way home to go walking as it was a beautiful day. But as we drove home I felt something strange happening to me and I went into vision.

In the sky she could see the vortex sweeping the earth and the universe in front of her. Incredibly majestic it was collecting energy from all of nature around it. Then she saw a second vortex sweep through the heavens and they came together to dance, to part and come together again. It was magnificent.

Suddenly I started having extreme difficulty breathing and my husband took me home as quickly as possible and arranged an urgent visit for me at the surgery. The doctor diagnosed I was not absorbing any oxygen and sent me to hospital into the critical care ward. My husband stayed with me until quite late and I gradually drifted into unconsciousness. I felt strangely at ease and that if I was going to die I had no need of anything from anybody, I could accept whatever was to happen. Everything around me faded, and I could feel myself sinking into a welcoming velvety blackness. My last thought was that I was dying, whereupon I felt an intensity of deep Love and I let go everything.

The World of Death, the Passion

She became acutely aware of entering another world. It was very striking. In the blackness she perceived the same cowled forms she had seen in the earth Womb but here they had black cloaks and flaming spiritual eyes. She floated among them and they criss-crossed in front of her awareness in acknowledgement of her presence. She went deep into the blackness, a strange world where she could see burning the black fires of purification and Love. She knew she was travelling through the world of death and it was exquisite, captivating her consciousness with its irresistible power, pulling her down to a sea of swelling velvety blackness; she felt at rest and in peace.

Suddenly her awareness was projected to a different place. She could see the two worlds conjoined; the hospital ward and the death world were as one in her consciousness and she floated between them both, for a short time suspended between the two. Then she felt a powerful energy cut into her upper chest and move down through her body like hot ice, down into the very depths of her being to meet there with an intense energy. Her body then experienced a joyous acknowledgement and the icy hot energy rose up, cutting back up through her body, up to her chest. An overwhelming feeling of deep passion burned throughout her body cracking it with an immense movement like a fragmented eggshell. She was enraptured and consumed by the passion.

The Yin Yang

Then her vision widened to a greater perspective. From a point deep within the universe she could see two great lakes of liquid energy in constant movement. One giving, the other receiving, each yielding and then returning the flow; each the reciprocal of the other, in acknowledgement of the universal flow of eternal Love. She was embodying the same principle she had seen earlier, the two great vortices dancing together in the sky. The feeling became intense and she moved back into the world of death, back to the cowled forms to be taken even deeper.

The Revealer was with me throughout, keeping my mind alert and conscious, speaking to me of holding Love in stillness. He explained that the creator is always looking into the creation to find a body sufficiently empty of past and time to fill with the seeds of life. The flame then fills the body, expanding to keep the body pure, allowing it to become the sacred area of pure Love into which the seeds of all nature are gently planted and fertilised.

In death you carry these seeds within you in the sacred flame to enter into the centre of the earth where God holds and keeps the divine vessel with your beloved opposite contained within, the first energised body between the two worlds. He awaits those few who can make the crossing in death and for those few in life who are prepared to die for the creation. It is difficult for people to know their own creation for only a few achieve it in conscious death. Only those who die consciously in the body can be aware of their creation at all times in life.

The Revealer explained I was now joined as one with my spiritual opposite and that my body is now inseparable from all life on the planet and that all life on earth comes through it. Impersonal cosmic Love through death made conscious is living intelligence, plasma the living matter of all cells. It is felt in the body as a fluid feeling, a sublime feeling of living intelligence moving about the body, from the lover back to the beloved joining them together as one body with the divine.

The Revealer told me not to be afraid for He is always with me. My mind was dying to my past reality and He would keep me aware and conscious and fill my mind with the laws of Love, for I was to learn much of conscious dying, human Love and spiritual laws. He advised me to let go of this life, for spiritually there was more I needed to do after going through the death barrier. He reassured me that I would be safe, as He had encased my body in a new orbital energy so it would not crack, wither or die and the doctors and nurses would do the rest. Then He told me to rest, as He would show me more.

Dying into Love, the Back Flame

When I woke the next morning my husband was with me. I slept most of the next day. That night when everyone had settled down I drifted into sleep and became immediately aware of the world of death. I was at peace. My awareness was projected out into the ward to the critically ill patients lying in their beds around me.

She could see the burning black fires of purification and Love transforming the death energy of the dying people around her. The black fires began to change colour and form into sparkling multicoloured flames flickering around their bodies engulfing them. She was thrust back into her body to feel again the searing energy cut through her and she felt consumed by a deep and sublime passion. This passion drew enough Love towards her to sustain her in death as in life, both sides in

141

balance. Instinctively she knew she was dying but this time dying into Love. God's Love was so welcoming, she could not leave it, there was no choice in the matter and she had no care. Then her body opened again and she could feel energy pouring into it. Some of the dying people walked towards her in their spiritual form holding the different coloured flames in their hands and they poured them into her upper body.

I came through that night to wake up in the hospital ward wondering when it would all end. I spoke to my husband about my fears of dying without seeing the rest of my family, but I could not reveal to him my visions and experience. But the nurses and doctors tending me felt the power of the stillness and commented on it. As night drew near I returned to the deep place of the death world and I felt the passion begin again.

Impersonal Love

Friends she had known and people she did not know visited her in their spiritual bodies, bringing their Love in the form of a flame, which they dropped into her body. She was being shown the power of impersonal spiritual and Divine Love. All the Love she had given to others in her lifetime was now coming back to her in a way she could not have imagined. Demonstration that it matters not how or where you give your Love, it will be returned to you. Not necessarily through the same people, as often you would wish, but through others you may not even know. Demonstration that all life is as one, beyond our limited mental understanding.

When we really know this as a spiritual law all crying ceases. The person you Love may turn away from you or leave, but Love can not and will not leave you. I have made my life a life of Love as I had always intended. The Love I was dying into was the magnificence of God's Love for all people. Barry and my husband had activated and grounded this Love in me bringing it into the physical world and now I had to live it. I was not allowed to give up my responsibility to bring Love into the world by escaping into the divine Love through physical death. Love was made fully conscious in me; Love would not let me go and the power of it increased over the weeks that followed.

A week later the man opposite me died and I felt much love come through to me from him. In its impersonal nature this represents the outer experience of the Love I had felt for my father maybe because I had been kept from him in his last days. The passion was becoming overwhelming and I longed to be united with it permanently but this was not allowed for I was continually brought back to the physical world. I remained in a critical state for a week before they were able to stabilise me and I was sent home. I could see that the Love around me was drawing me back into the world. I was bringing death to life and the two worlds were closer now.

Chapter xxvi

Stillness

There was a profound stillness in me, which everyone at home could feel. I had descended into a place of mystery. My family and friends supported me and with their Love the passion would start again. It continued for several weeks and I was not able to move. All thinking had stopped, and when anyone wanted to converse with me, I communicated in vision from that place of stillness, where I was being kept without thought. There was always a soft breeze in the room.

She was behind a wall of blue flames, and through the flames she could see a giant vortex of energy, with the world at the very top of the vortex. The physical world was at a standstill, and she knew that this would come to pass in the future, the world suspended in time, in stillness. With all peoples minds stopped, for how long no one would know, we would move into a new dimension, a new universal consciousness, and like stepping through a doorway the transition would be easy. And she knew that we would need to build a new body for this future world, whilst still in the old.

As she continued to look, she could see all people are linked. Each with millions of black lines within, leading from their solar-plexus to other bodies, connecting them through the link of emotion to everyone that has ever lived. With some people this line has broken and she could see them speeding down the vortex towards her and beyond to be lost forever in the void.

I was there behind the blue flames in timeless consciousness with my physical body in time. I was in such a deep spiritual state that if I lived the vision or put my attention fully on the mystery within I would lose form and disappear as witnessed sometimes by my friends. I was learning the difference between being in the body and out of it. I felt very strange and it took me months to recover.

For several weeks I stayed in deep peace. Looking out of the window I watched the play of energies in nature. The screen of flames I had descended behind had become more translucent. But I would catch the odd flicker from time to time, reminding me of where I was. Nothing was solid; I was seeing all life as a liquid energy. Even the room would seem to disappear in front of me. Life would manifest first in the flame, then in liquid and then in solid form.

Trying to maintain my hold on reality one morning, I saw some birds gradually coming to life on the bedroom windowsill before my very eyes. When I blinked they would be gone again, dematerialising and then reforming. I was being shown, through the realisation of Love, the spiritual truth that nothing is solid and the entire physical world is just a projection from the human body and mind. I had no idea that Love was so masterful and commanding. Love made and built the natural world. This is the real Love that we instinctively know ourselves to be deep inside our bodies. I had done what Barry Long said was impossible: the two principles were now firmly rooted in me and the feeling was exquisite.

As I was to find out I was being prepared again for the breath of life behind time and into eternity. As I watched the blue flame expanded and the Revealer stepped out to explain that I had laid a good foundation in the physical world for Love to flood into and that without the Love it would have been impossible for me to return. The next part of my development was to be mostly in vision to show me how the balance between the two worlds would be maintained in my body, prepared and preserved through Love and cosmic intervention. In my eyes, a miracle had taken place, but I was to see that nothing was impossible when the intelligence of spiritual Love works with you.

Holðing to Life

My husband decided to take me for a drive in the countryside to get me accustomed to the outside world. It felt very strange. As he drove faster, instead of rushing past, the visible world appeared to fold up and collapse in a sequence of still frames and disappear inside my body; swallowed as if by a tunnel. I was being shown that all life emanates and is formed from the human body via the mind. This is the truth behind premonitions, deja-vu and other projected phenomena. All of life is in the past, we live in a projected reality which has already been lived inside our minds. The brain has created everything in the material world.

I drifted into sleep and on arrival awoke feeling refreshed. We had driven to a hilltop with spectacular views of the surrounding countryside. It was one of those beautiful days where you want to be at one with nature for as long as possible. I mentioned to my husband my strange tunnel like vision. We walked into a wooded area where it was cooler, in the hope that I might regain more normal sight. I appreciated how lovely it was but I still could not see the whole of the scene in front of me and wherever I tried to focus I felt a little unsafe, so we stopped for a while to rest.

Walking back through the wood I could see only a few yards in front of me. My focus seemed to project rapidly forward, ricochet off the sun energy field and then rush back at me. Around the edge of my view was a mist of energy aura. I was seeing creation in slow motion. It was evident to me that my own projected image was weak and I realised the fact that where there is no projection there is no life in the outside world. I could see more life if I descended down into my body, which I could not sustain a moment longer. I sat down on the grass and withdrew into the life within.

Life was teeming within her body. She came across the same hilltop and wooded landscape she had projected outside of her. Then she encountered the giant vortex that pulled her further into her body, transporting her to another dimension, the angelic kingdom and it was beautiful. She could see millions of angelic beings coming together to form a human body which she recognised as her own. She realised her own physical body was dematerialising which was why she had no hold on life. Remembering what the Revealer had said to her, she knew eventually the body would reform and that everything would be all right.

I told my husband it was time to go home. I felt very detached and it was days before I could retain normal sight. I took short walks near my home and gradually it improved.

Chapter xxvii

The Black Red Flame, the Reconstitution of Matter

The Revealer took her to the black red flame burning fiercely in the earth Womb. The spiritual forms were cloaked so she could see them and their eyes glowed brightly with spiritual fire. They were working on the containment of the energy of dead matter that comes through the part of the mind that has been made conscious at the time of death. Having served its purpose as memory in the world there is no more use for it. It has no further use as memorable past coming into the present so can not dictate the future; as the fully conscious being is filled with Love no past can enter in. Now obsolete and ready for reconstitution it is poured into the spiritual flames.

She saw before her the dead matter in the form of millions of dead bodies. Looking more closely she could see a spark of compacted essence being gathered from each dead body like the kernel of a nut being removed from the shell. And she saw the division of the two energies, the spark and the dead matter, dividing and following their separate courses. More and more matter was pushed into the black red fire for the gathering of conscious energy, and the sparks came together and ignited to create the magnificent eternal blue flame. She could feel its pervasive Godly power.

The Revealer explained to her that this was the demonstration that each body before her, as dead matter and memory, had been made conscious. He went on to say these substances make up the shadow and are thrust into the world by the thinking mind. Every one of us has the potential in our subconscious minds to hold and make it conscious in our lifetime; this helps to build our new body. Those people who psychologically build a wall around themselves to avoid having to deal with this during life are confronted with it at the time of their death, there is no escape.

The red black fire raged as the dead matter was consumed within it and the element of the eternal blue flame besid0e it burned brilliantly. She watched in fascination as it began to move, passing between the Revealer and her own spiritual body consuming the dead matter within her physical body. With the Revealer she was drawn to the blue pillar of fire and the black red flame passed through them and united them with the pillar. With the gathering of conscious energy she was renewed. The Revealer had come to her side again in His unrelenting Love for her to show her the next stage of her physical renewal, proving that all life is eternal.

He moved closer to reassure her pointing to the red black flame and in the sparks of the fire she saw union with the spiritual male and female. Myriad's of tiny multicoloured sparks danced above them, gathering to form a sparkling display of the union of opposite colours binding together to create countless tiny vortices. The vortices then combined to form a waxy energetic substance, an intelligence that transposed into a DNA like structure. It circled around them at great speed in recognition and acknowledgement of their presence and the speed of its revolutions gradually slowed until it finally came to a halt directly in front of them, changing form for the last time into an aqua flame.

The flames continued to dance towards the DNA like structure as I watched and I felt I had known all this before instinctively. Having made the psychic energy conscious in my mind over the years my body had now gone through the death barrier. The Revealer beckoned to me and satisfied that He had shown me all to put my mind at rest concerning the death energies, we parted.

Gathering Life Energy

The Revealer had taken me back into the earth Womb to reveal how the reconstitution of old worn out matter in the form of memory had been taken out of the old body I currently inhabited, back into the whole to give it new life. I had been shown that everything that happens in the mind gathers the past. And that the spiritual person must endeavour to make every part of their life conscious by gathering the minute particles of compacted energy of the life spark that makes everything in life operate. When there is no more use for the past the energy required can be extracted from the dead matter of the body to build the new body in the life- to death in the life cycle.

This is also how the physical body is kept pure beyond death in life now. There is decay in all matter, which eventually takes us to our death. The decay, which is past flooding out from the subconscious and activating every atom in the body, eventually causes the body to decay and die. It is a natural cycle in this world as is demonstrated around us. But even whilst we are a thinking and reasonably healthy person this can still cause us great distress. It gravitates into the body to form an immovable inert mass. Dead matter is responsible for all manner of ill health if not contained within the puri- fying flame of transforming energy.

But it is possible to guide some highly conscious people to ignite their own flame for regeneration without projecting their dead matter into the outside world without the repercussions through karmic law. The few who make it through the death barrier of the body, while still alive, are those who have been fully conscious through death while their new body is being formed, enabling them to move from the

150

physical to their new body without any loss of conscious awareness. They can then have the pleasure of an extended life on this planet and are now in a position to relay spiritual knowledge back to people from behind time.

They can be taken directly to the Golden Age with mental ease and with no break in that wonderful consciousness they already know. Union with the opposite is the doorway for both male and female regardless of what has been taught as an intellectual belief. This lack of union and consciousness is the reason why most people die in ignorance and suffering and do not know the beauty of the earth and its connection to Love and the Womb. Woman creates this earth with God through her Womb with the pure Love of man. This is their divine purpose and ecstasy ensuring the survival of the creation. Man can only master the creation when he is truly in union with these principles. For when man is in his mental capacity only he disconnects himself from the creation and its purpose to sustain life from here to eternity.

Chapter xxviii

The Aqua Flame of Cell Regeneration

This is the fire that holds, protects and maintains the physical body while it is purified and transformed in the other flames. It is the flame of cell regeneration. As we take in dead cells from the atmosphere they are purified in the other flames and reconstituted back into the body through the aqua flame. This flame holds the psychic and mental renewal for all those people who pass beyond death and stay beyond death in a physical body. Without the aqua flame's protection this would not be possible.

She looked into the aqua flame in amazement. At first she could not understand what she saw but over the months that passed as the Revealer took her deeper into the flame, she could see the skeletal structure of a female body. Then she realised it was her own; that she was observing the creation of her new spiritual body and she was drawn to it like a magnet. The fire would gently but firmly caress the skeleton, each flame folding and forging to form layers like molten wax around the contours of the structure.

Finally she could see her body completely renewed within the fire, but as her body instinctively rose and tried to break out of the fire the cowled forms circled around her forming a barrier to keep her within.

The fascination of seeing this had a great effect on me mentally. I was being told spiritually that all was well, confirmation was received through vision that my health would return. As the weeks went by I wondered what would be the catalyst for the release of my new body. Then I saw it.

Looking at the Love being gathered in my body, where it is being made at all times; I saw a portion splinter off in the form of a flame. The cowled forms stepped aside from the aqua flame to allow the Love to encircle it. The newly formed body moved forward into the flame of Love and was transported within it to the centre of my physical body. The flame dispersed within, changing the DNA throughout its cellular structure, continually preparing my body for the earth spirit consciousness.

The Capsule

I had only known Andi for six months. She attended a series of workshops I was running and came to our group meeting a couple of times. When she heard I was ill she come to help. She suggested doing some crystal healing and immediately she started I went into vision.

Up she travelled through a crystal vortex to find herself inside a capsule within a spacecraft, once again in the hands of cowled cosmic beings. She saw they had removed their cloaks revealing their form to be much like her own, only more transparent. She sensed their unique intelligence as they slid open the capsule cover and began to operate on her lungs, removing them from her body for inspection to a small table with a tray of illuminated crystals beneath. They pressed some control buttons and the lungs disappeared inside the crystal display screen.

Meanwhile she could feel her body being continually regenerated by an energy that surrounded her like millions of tiny intelligent vibrating crystals. She could sense the beings communicating with each other and an overseer, who seemed to be monitoring the whole process, telepathically reassured her that all was well. She felt very safe.

They finished their work and the crystal screen was transferred over to her capsule and her renewed breathing apparatus lowered back into her chest. Her capsule was then closed with her inside it and sent at high speed through a vacuum tube to a launch pad, then ejected from the spaceship and launched into deep space. She could see the stars and planets rushing towards her and nearing the earth the most spectacular and beautiful patterns of colour and the pulsating of the universe.

The Indian Song

When her awareness next returned she was back on earth with woodland all around. Her body was partially submerged in the soft earth and stood over her was an American Indian. He was not wearing anything to suggest he was in any way special, but as she watched he walked over to a tree and snapped a branch with two protruding twigs extending from it. In his pocket he had a leather thong and a stone tool. Positioning the branch between his knees he proceeded to create an opening in the branch and insert the leather thong through it. Having completed the hollow channel through the branch he held it up to the light.

Then the Indian laid the branch on his arm with the forked end over his hand and softly began to sing to Mother earth to bring the wood alive. The haunting sounds touched and stirred her in a way she had not known before and her body seemed to come alive. The song was more than mere notes. It resonated with all life, demonstrating to her that she was a part of nature.

He stroked the branch and, responding to his touch and song, it softened in his hand taking on the form of a human bronchial tube. Walking over to her, he knelt by her side and lowered it into her chest. And then he sang a new song as this living part of the natural earth moulded with her. He held out his hand to her as she rose out of the earth and walked her to a nearby stream where he lowered her in and she floated away. When she looked back he was gone.

I returned to the room and told my friend about my mysterious adventure. I realised that because the mental and spiritual energies were in correct balance within me, with the union of the cosmic and earth energies; profound healing had taken place.

The feeling of Love conveyed to me in both these visions was a testament to cosmic and spiritual Law. It showed me all was well, I was slowly recovering and that I should trust in what I had seen and experienced. I had been shown that the two sides of my physical and spiritual worlds were unified and in balance. The Love I was receiving from my spiritual friends and my husband resulted in more clarity and knowledge accompanied by vision.

I was to realise that the pure male principle, eternally within you, can and will take on any form acceptable to your mind in any situation. It offers you eternal Love to unify the opposites within you and outside in the physical world, if you can reach and join with spiritual Love while in the physical body in your life. The letter from Barry in which he had talked of the sixth and last sense, which is the human body, meant much more now. And he was arriving in England in a couple of month's time.

Chapter xxix

The Fig and the Blood

Never ask a spiritual Master anything unless you can deal with the answer for every spiritual law has to be lived to be understood. In a recent letter I had asked Barry about the true nature of the opposites vortices, the pure compacted essence inside the body, which I had experienced. I was about to go into the full power and knowledge of what I had lived, as energy forming, shown to me in the Garden of Love.

She was woken one day by the sun streaming in the window and the lovely sound of the birds in the garden. Cherishing the early morning she lay there for a few moments taking in the beauty and it drew her into the Garden of Love inside her body.

She could see Adam still tending to Eve (The name Adam in Hebrew means red earth). She looked wide-awake now and he was a glorious sight showing her the same tender Love and care as in the beginning when he had taken her out from the earth. He carried her everywhere around the Garden, which was vast and down to the stream to bathe her. She could see and feel the Love between them. Eve would drape herself around his body and it was effortless for him to care for her. As she grew stronger he was able to leave her for a short time and to protect her whilst he was gone, he left her with the serpent energy that watched over her in the Garden.

Then she saw Eve sitting under a tree whilst he gathered more fruit for her to eat. He returned and handed her a fig. As Eve bit into it her face changed and at the same time she felt a great change in her own body. Something was not right. Whilst Adam stood there looking at her Eve began to shiver. The fig was dripping blood, sacred blood; it ran down her arms and onto her body. She looked devastated for she knew what was happening was not good. She sat frozen to the spot while the blood dripped all over her until it covered her completely and then entered into her beautiful waxen body. The body of Love, the pure feeling of the pure flesh that is sustained by the movement of Love from the loved one back to the beloved.

The sacred blood, her life energy from all creation, was now mixed with a substance not so pure. Adam had given her some of his emotion, from his thinking mind, which her body was trying to reject. With the emotion entering Eve, the spiritual silence was interrupted, the movement of the loved one back to the beloved ceased. Emotion now in her pure mind and being alien to her nature, she experienced fear, putting her into shock. She has been in shock ever since and woman needs to come out of this state.

Given the experience of the pure flesh of woman and the understanding in his mind of how God loved her so completely, with her purpose in creation, Adam wished to covet her Love and usurp the place of God. He wished to create his world with the physical woman making her for himself. He proceeded to make a replica through his mind of himself first and then woman. This was the first thought of self and selfishness coming into being. This was the second creation.

Adam gave his emotion and thoughts to Eve to make her body more solid to protect her in the outside world that he wished to create for himself. But it works in reverse, for emotion draws to itself its own reflection from the outside world of experience. In his intention to protect her, the sacred blood was polluted and the movement of the pure flesh to join couples in the

*timeless union of Love was stopped. From that time on, man
could no longer be joined to the Love he so craved and desired.
He had chosen to usurp the power of the Almighty, thinking he
knew the laws of life better than God. He should have left it to
God for in reality the blockage of Love causes great suffering to
lovers as they frantically try to reach each other.*

*The fig that Eve had been holding took on new life. It began to
pulse and she looked at Adam in bewilderment. He knelt
down to guide and shows her where to place it in her body.
Her malleable form yielded to the weight of the fig, which sank
into her to form the Womb of creation in the new world.*

Not satisfied to stay encased in his divine body, linked with
God and unified with pure Love. Adam took on an alien mind
and made a replica body of woman, which he projected out of
his body to enable him to experience it for himself on the
outside, separate from God. He was aware of the intelligence
of life moving on the outside in the garden and his desire was
to move into it to have the mirror of the Love he desired.
Totally encased in the Love inside the womb of the earth,
unified with her opposite and possessing no mind herself, Eve
had no wish to move into an outside alien world. Adam knew
that ejected outside of his body she would experience suffering
from his world, but whichever world he wished for, he knew
Eve in her selfless Love would create it through her Womb
(the pure essence inside the replica body) to encapsulate and
sustain him in his new world.

The Voice of God

*Then the presence of a voice was heard in the garden, an all
pervading infinite energy communicating the disdain a parent
feels when children have been caught doing something
contrary to the guiding Love of infinite wisdom.*

Adam and Eve looked at each other and then in the direction of the voice. The voice and the energy closed in on the couple encircling them as they drew closer together. Adam tried to hide Eve and what he had done to her; Eve, the body of pure Love, pure flesh, the divine Love of God, who had taken on this emotion unwittingly. Then the infinite energy of God offered her back the purity to enable her to enter back into the body of Adam and both to enter the womb of the earth through the Garden. But now, like Adam, she could think and wishing to stay with her loved one to create for him whatever he wanted in the physical world, she felt choiceless. No matter what she had to go through, her Love, her man needed her. Willingly Eve chose to leave the Garden of Love.

Eve was too sacred to enter the world as she was in the pure flesh in the Garden, so Adam had to make a replica of her from his own body and with the help of the animals her new body formed, which is what woman is today. Through the sound of the voice, the infinite energy of God moved around her, moulding her new body through its vibrations. The beautiful waxen body of flesh was left in the Garden and a more solid body was formed from the matter of nature. Small animals collected grasses to lay on her body that fused together to circulate the blood around her body and then into the new Womb. Gracefully walking towards her an antelope brought her a rose for a heart. In an act of consciousness all the animals and the birds flying down from the trees brought the varied aspects of nature to gently build her body.

Thus the energy from the life around her, the pristine beauty of nature was instilled in her body. For God allowed her to keep a portion of the divine Love compacted in her Womb enabling her and her Love, Adam, to keep the creation in perfection connected to God through their Love for each other. Adam's body too became heavier and much more solid. Then the vibrations of the voice energy picked up the serpent energy from the garden and transferred it to Adam's body containing it in the penis from where it had come, enabling him to enter Eve in physical Love as he craved to do.

Projected out of the penis the serpent energy, the pure male principle of Love, was degraded, it became filled with emotion and time. Adam had the power to return Eve back to purity through pure Love without emotion but he chose instead to experience emotion and use it to construct his world, projected by force out from his mind. The serpent left its rightful place within the penis and in the form of the snake tried to beguile Eve from within the physical form of Adam, which is man today. And he succeeded.

"Because you have done this you are the cursed of all the domestic animals. And of all the wild beasts of the field upon your belly you will go and dust you will eat all the days of your life." (Genesis 3.14)

Honour The Womb

With their bodies completely formed, again the voice was heard. It came as a swirling vortex that gripped and sustained their bodies. Adam and Eve held on to each other as the vortex propelled them out of the Garden to the veil between worlds. As they passed through, the veil enclosed their forms in a translucent like substance, and its purity was extracted to form the flames of compacted sacred energy. Buried deep within the solar plexus this energy completed their new bodies carrying within them the sacred laws to the new land. They looked back to see the Garden fade away. All that remained were the Seraphim angels with their fiery swords. Then Eve poured out into his new world all of the Garden and the creation contained within her Womb so that Adam could have the delight of her, the beauty that is woman, all around him.

Man has chosen this constructed world for himself. He has deserted the true creation in favour of his own intellectually constructed world. And woman, the reflection of his disconnection with true Love, wanders the wilderness of his loveless world crying for the Love that she instinctively knows and yearns for, the true Love that man wilfully denies her.

Today, man and woman have come so far from what true divine Love represents that it is almost impossible to reach it through each other. For only when they truly love, banishing all thought of self, can they be reunited with Love. But in his deep psyche man knows his is a world of selfishness, but he feels it is too hard to give up his self and re-connect with his pure principle of woman and pure Love. Woman is at the mercy of man and the transience of his Love, until the time she realises the truth of divine Love and is permanently drawn back to the earth spirit, reunited with the eternal male through the Love of the Creator.

When man disconnects himself from his Love, woman, in her divine mystery she then has the power to move with the Creator. Woman can isolate herself from man sufficiently to purify her body and mind through the Creators love enabling her to re-connect with her opposite, the pure principle of man held between the worlds by God. Then she is united with the whole of creation, no gap in time, with the living intelligence of all life. Then she can consciously bring pure living matter, all of life through her physical Womb and into this creation.

So God has stepped in for woman in place of man. When Adam chose to leave the Garden, the omnipotent all knowing power of God kept with Him the essence of woman, the divine principle of woman. Her conscious connection back to God is ensured now, if she will give herself to the earth spirit of creation. This means, she will be in peace and love before her body dies, giving her the power to die into Divine love no matter what her circumstances. This is her right. For the creator knows that purity, Love without thought, is the truth of all life and that woman needs to connect with the divine

Love of God above all else. Only then can man be brought back to his true nature of pure Love.

This is the truth of the triangle of divine Love, the Holy Trinity; God - the omnipotent; the son - all of mankind; the Holy Ghost - the Love that is made through the opposites. In physical reality by man and woman, creating the pure Spirit, the sacredness of love that is real woman in her purity. The spiritual creative womb, replenishing the mystery of the creation. God then works with man of love through the Womb of woman giving her the power to create all life eternally.
The pure principle of man, in the form of solar energy nurtures the earth Womb, the creation by giving warmth and nourishment. When man and woman are physically cut off from each other, without the grounding of pure Love through physical lovemaking and union linking them to the divine for the manifestation of all life, nothing can come into creation.

Women know what you are and honour your Womb above all else. It is time for woman to draw everything back into her Womb to build her new world of Love with her beloved. Man can generate enormous power for life by activating in her and himself the solar atom through love making, generating the matrix of all life, the figure of eight movement from heart to Womb drawing all life through their bodies, replenishing the creation. Thus purified, their spirit bodies float into the sacred lands of the spirit to unite with God in divine love. Returning through the veil of time, man carries woman back into the Garden to unite with the passion of God; complete fulfilment.

The Ageless Womb
Wrapped around my tiny Womb,
The world is spinning, cradling its web.

Weaving, rocking, from ages past,
It's timeless union though mountains pass,
Keeping rhythm, through sun and moon,
Pulled to earth to help her birth.

When all is lined in perfect balance,
She bursts forth in exaltation.
Throwing forth another web,
Keeping earth replenished with life.

Chapter xxx

Eternity

A friend invited me to visit her, it was mid July and very hot. I had not done much since coming out of hospital but I decided it was time to do more, so I went. It was always a pleasure to visit her. Our in depth exchanges of spiritual knowledge always seemed to activate something profound in me and this day was no exception. After a swim and lunch we sat down to talk. Looking at the flowing waters of the Thames I wondered at how I had gone beyond physical death and gathered universal Love and my friend remarked that there was never an end to the mystery. I felt a little uneasy as if I was soon to find out, could I take any more deep encounters with the spirit.

The sun shining on the water transported her to a place of exquisite spiritual beauty filled with angels of such splendour, tall as the trees and standing so still. She watched in wonder as legions of more angels came through the sky, wielding their fiery swords in execution of the law. They circled around the motionless angels and pointed their swords into their midst to create a magnificent point of entry.

She was drawn irresistibly into the flame combined of magenta violet, the pink flame of pure Love and the cobalt blue flame of the divine will each yielding to the other. She felt humbled by its magnificence and majesty and by the unmissable knowledge that here she was entering God in full consciousness. The flame carried above it an orb containing the infinite atom, the point of creation, carrying within a universal law as yet unknown which was dropped into her spirit body for metamorphosis in her physical reality. A silent vow between her and God, her acquiescence to her place in the creation to come into being.

I was brought back into the garden with my friend but it was just too beautiful to speak of. After I had sufficiently gained my grasp of reality I thanked her saying my goodbyes and went home driving along the rural back roads to maintain the presence, for I wanted to stay with the beauty. Sitting in the garden having supper that evening with my husband and daughter I felt the unmistakable feeling of the all pervasive power of stillness that comes with deep union with the spirit. I said my goodnights to my family and went to bed and immediately fell into a deep sleep. All of a sudden I woke with a start; it felt like my whole body was being ripped apart from top to bottom and the pain was so severe I became unconscious momentarily.

Entering Into the Opposite

She descended back down among the stillness of angels, through the spirit fire in their midst and down into the Garden of Love. She was at peace. She lay on the earth and sank into its yielding warmth.

In the distance she saw the formless body of divine man, a shimmering mirage of the creational energies, the sun, the moon and the stars moving within. The intelligence of all life moving towards her and she yielded to it. In recognition, the pure feeling then moved in her linking her sublimely to her divine opposite through the earth, putting her spiritual and physical bodies into deep peace.

He came over to her and knelt at her side. He reached over her body and ripped it open from bottom to top to lift out a pure golden body, a tiny spiritual duplicate of her own and he drew it towards him. She was just big enough to stand in his cupped hands and he walked away with her to another part of the garden. She looked back at her worn out body laid on the earth, a lifeless replica of what she had been.

He then looked into her eyes and she could feel the powerful magnetic union between them burning within. Her small golden body softened like molten wax and burst into flickers of spiritual fire and like a waxen candle was consumed by the fires until all that remained of her was a tiny flame burning in each of his hands. He drew the flames of her essence into his upper body and in spirit form she was returned to her beloved. She had given everything to God, man, and life and in doing so she was brought back into physical life.

All was perfection and the sense of completeness at times was overwhelming as she watched the spiritual and physical worlds coalesce. She could see everything come alive before her eyes and she felt the complete harmony and endless beauty of it all. Unified with the principle of man throughout the earth, she had found her opposite in Love, the union all people are seeking on this earth. She had found her way home to eternity. The place of infinite stillness without beginning or end, unlimited by time where everything dematerialises before it even happens in the physical world. This was the breath behind time.

Whispers

The flame that flickers ever bright,
Opens in your heart by night,
Whispers within of God's new plan,
Preparing you for the sacred land.

The land of Love that awaits you,
God's pleasure, the flame, to draw you through.

Cosmic power compacted in light,
Each fold carries a contrasted law,
Unmistakably flawless, unpredictable too.

Suspended in time by the spirit ever new,
Joined as one, to convey its mystery to you.

I had been shown my worn out, obsolete replica worldly body. It had done its job; it had brought me passion through this world of pain. I was being kept alive at the time by powerful drugs, but a question mark now hung over this continuing. I wondered how long I could hold my body together. Somehow I knew if I could keep the balance between the inner and outer life, to close the gap between the two worlds sufficiently, I might be able to stay on the earth.

The Revealer came to me, reminding me of the orbital energy he had put around my body when I had gone through the time barrier. He told me "to embody the opposite principles life and death unite, bringing forth the power of spiritual Love to sustain corruptible matter for as long as the Divine wishes".

I kept the healing vision, which I had been shown in my mind, in the hope that it meant I would be sustained and healed. But in my deep state of peace it was hard to worry in any way. The following weeks were still and enjoyable. People helped me with their visits and by the time Barry had returned to England I felt well enough to drive to Bristol to see him and ask if he could cast any light on my spiritual experiences.

The Meeting

The evening I arrived I asked him publicly about interfacing the spiritual world with the physical. He queried my need to ask him anything, as I was the Yogini. At breakfast the next morning he came to speak to me privately and answered most of my questions, putting my mind at rest. I did not have time to mention my last big experience of uniting with spiritual man, but that afternoon his talk was about Love and it reminded me of my own experience in the garden and I spoke to Barry of my vision. Leaning towards me he sighed in the recognition of it, exclaiming "Oh, that is eternity". He stood and explained to the audience that my body had been broken down by psychic energy, that I had brought all life through it and now it had no further use. This was disturbing to hear because I desired to stay alive but I did not have another chance to talk with him further. The Revealer was around me and I felt a soft breeze as He came into my vision and I felt comforted.

Reflections In Time

That night, feeling somewhat distressed, I retired to bed. It was not long before the Revealer came to me and told me not to be afraid. As He washed my body in flashes of light He spoke to me of the renewal of my life, for this was why I was born. I had been shown in vision how the body dies into the divine opposite, so I would know in the future how to help and sustain others who also went through it and wished to stay on the Earth.

He went on to explain to me that our bodies are only reflections in time from the centre of the earth. The body, the shell, is dependent on the opposite partner sustaining it for as long as he or she can hold the image, with the still centre of love within. Where there is profound spiritual Love between them, the image of self, the body, dissolves so the Love can flood out to the opposite and the partner then has to try and hold the two together.

Where enough Love has been gathered in the body through lovemaking the power of divine Love will fill the image and the lovers move back behind time, through Love and over the death barrier to unite with the purity of true Love in God. If there is enough Love in the body image, they will be filled ceaselessly, and continue to live in time as living Love, for Love keeps the dying body clean enough to live in this corruptible world. The Revealer said He would teach me more about impersonal, cosmic and spiritual Love and its operation in the world. For those people who desired, I was to prepare for the time barrier and for Paradise.

Chapter xxxi

White Buffalo

Within the spiritual world I was becoming increasingly aware of the power of spiritual Love in all its glory and eternal power to demonstrate its supremacy of unique universal consciousness. My life was becoming more wondrous as the Revealer helped me to let go of the physical world. The more knowledge I was given through vision, the more I was shown the expanse and fullness of life that had been suppressed and denied to me and all people. The Revealer explained that he would show me the beauty of the whole of life, the divine web that connects us all. I wondered how much more my mind could take, He assured me all was well and to leave it in his safe hands. My next splendid encounter was when the Revealer walked me into the Native American Indians sacred grounds.

An eagle lifted her on its wings and took her to the world of the American Indians. She was dropped from the sky and through the clouds to where a ceremony was taking place; to where a medicine man was dancing the dance of revival to call the spirits to the Happy Hunting Ground. He welcomed her and led her up a long canyon, which spiralled like a snake, ending with huge mountains towering above.

At the foot of the mountains was a cave into which the medicine man disappeared and she followed him in. He went up to a woman dressed in soft skins, with beautiful beads around her neck and her braided hair adorned with feathers, flowers and bone amulets. They looked at each other with a deep knowing. Then he stepped back and she began to sing a haunting song of deep feeling pleading to the earth Mother. She clasped her hands to her body and rocked back and forth in profound lament for the beauty of the earth. Pleading the earth to release the spirits to her, those Indians that had died without rite of passage.

As they watched the top of the cave cracked and with an almighty movement the earth opened above them. Brilliant light streamed forth and a massive orb of light descended to hover in suspension between them. The Indian came back into the sunlight with a feather and beaded stick, which he proceeded to shake.

At the burial ground, the spirits of the dead rose creating a vortex of great earth spirit power and majesty, which swept the sky. The medicine man started to sing and chant and dance and she became aware of a thunderous noise as the orb of light moved into the centre of the vortex and rose up with it into the skies.

Soaring over the mountains the eagle carried her to a vast plateau where thousands of buffalo were stampeding and she could feel the ground shake as they drew near. They charged past at such a speed they were hidden in a cloud of dust. Then she saw a glowing form coming towards her that shimmered in the sunlight and seemed to block out all light as it moved closer. As it got nearer, she saw it was a white buffalo. It had broken away from the herd and was now walking gently towards her with such grace and majesty she felt dwarfed and humbled by its magnificent presence.

She looked closely at the buffalo and there was a look of communication in its eye. She stroked its head and ran her fingers down its neck and she saw it had been wounded from a broken arrow in his side. She removed the arrow but the wound was deep and she kept her hand over it whilst she stroked it for a while. She felt a scintillating warmth and vibration coming over her in waves and she saw, the vortex carrying the spirits of the resurrected Indians she had seen earlier at the burial ground reappeared.

Then she, the buffalo and the vortex with the orb within became one and sped off through the universe to enter a place of great wonder, the most beautifully silent place of rest with a light breeze in a land of perfection. Pristine natural beauty, in eternity. The land of the Happy Hunting Ground where the spirit of the land expresses its power and eternal rest in her body.

The vortex moved through this still land and in its intelligence gravitated to the heart of the land to drop the spirit of those that had lived on the earth into their Happy Hunting Ground. These were the spirits of Indians who had died unnatural deaths without the ceremony of the sacred rite of passage to lead them on their way into conscious death. The spirits can not be reincarnated as pure knowledge unless they are reinstated by spiritual burial in the Happy Hunting Ground. She saw the buffalo moving among them, honoured to be reunited with them.

The vortex then swooped down and placed the orb with the Indian spirits within it onto the ground. She watched in wonder as a circle of spiritual flame sprang up from the ground creating the crossover point from the spiritual realms into the physical earth. Creating the power to resurrect the spirits into physical bodies on the earth to continue the spiritual teachings and knowledge so that Mother Nature is protected and flourishes. Ensuring the web of all life stays inter- connected as one.

And in the stillness the elements of nature gathered there and the God of thunder whose voice was calm, the foremost overseer of the land moved forward to command where they should be placed. Then the God of wind gently rolling to and fro welcomed the spirit Indians, embracing them and giving support in acknowledgement of their return to the Happy Hunting Ground. Next the Gods of feeling gathered around and the rain poured down; their tears a profusion of dark blue liquid. Nearing the earth's atmosphere the droplets became more solid and she saw them drop into the earth and grow into the blue corn of the Indian nation. She was informed that when consumed by the Indians this pure corn would reconnect them with their heritage no matter how far away from it they had wandered.

This vision was a demonstration of universal consciousness and I was to experience many more remarkable insights on my spiritual journey. I wondered why I was being given truths from other cultures. I realised it was because we have become too detached from our own spiritual heritage through preference for rational and intellectual thought.

The Indian nations and others like them established their link with the spirit of Love and life long ago. The Great Earth Spirit of truth is being made conscious through those who died without ceremony, so they are resurrected in us to reconnect us to the earth spirit of all life. Later that year a native Red Indian told me a rare white buffalo had just been born in his land.

Chapter xxxii

The Golden Orb

On my return from the Barry Long course I explained to my husband the peace and equilibrium I had felt and commented on how good it would be to be with Barry for his four weeks master sessions in beautiful surroundings in Australia. Dave said if I felt so good about it I should go. I wondered at first if it was right for me to go but as always with anything major in my life, I knew I would sense or feel what was right. That night I descended into sleep feeling a profound feeling of warmth. I saw a golden ball of light and it took me into vision.

She was moving at immense speed across the earth over the countryside and towards the ocean. It was winter in England and she unfurled from the golden ball to stand on the cold shore. The sea was tumultuous but also inviting. She stood and gazed about her but was continually drawn back to the water. She enfolded herself back into the golden ball of light and descended deep into the ocean. Instinctively, she knew where she was going and before long surfaced to find herself on the golden sands of a tropical country. The scenery was breathtaking with a timeless quality. There were luxuriant forests she had never seen the like of before and beautiful flowers of deep lasting colours she had seen only in the Garden of Love.

Looking around, she saw something glisten in the sun light. It moved and came into view, the golden body of a man with his arms outstretched in her direction. She felt a powerful desire to unite with him that was overwhelming. He walked towards

174

her and reached out to pick her up and carried her in among
the trees and flowers. He held her whilst she looked around.
Together they blended with the natural energies and were
absorbed into the golden light of each other and she felt an
intense feeling of warmth and Love in her body.

I woke next morning with the feeling still in my body and I
knew I was to go to Australia. The vision had informed me of
this and knowing the integrity of spiritual law, I was sure I
would be able to go. I rang the Barry Long Foundation and
within five minutes everything was booked and arranged and
I had only a few weeks to prepare myself.

On my arrival I was pleasantly surprised to find I was booked
into a motel right on the beach. I was shown to my room with
a balcony that looked over white sands, palm trees, blue skies
and the sea. It was paradise and everything that I needed. I
showered, changed and went out to explore. It did not take
me long to meet a group of people I enjoyed being with during
my visit, many of whom have since become good friends. That
night exhausted with jet lag after the long flight I sank into a
deep sleep.

She was awoken by the sound of the sea lapping on the shore
and rising from her bed stepped outside to sit in the moonlight.
She sat there for a long while until she could see the golden
glow of the sunrise. But then she realised it was not the sun.
The golden man was standing there on the sand looking at her
for what seemed like eternity. She stood up and walked
towards him to reunite in the golden glow of warmth and Love
she had felt before, absorbed in its glorious energy.

For the next three days until the course started I was able to
absorb this energy and meet up with more people. Some of
them were friends from home and it was lovely to see them.
But at night it was good to return alone to the deep peace of
my room and the sound of the waves as I drifted into sleep.

Some nights I could hear the earth speaking to me. It seemed as if I was enveloped in the Womb of the great earth and my consciousness would roll with the waves.

The Dreamtime

She was running with grass and sand underfoot and ahead of her was a hill, which she began to climb; looking up into the sunlight she was startled by black figures rising over the hilltop. Their bodies shone a deep ebony in the sun and they had spears in their hands; a hunting party of Aboriginals. For a moment she could feel her heart beating with such intensity and fear she was almost shocked out of the vision, but she continued up the hill when hearing the soft voices of their haunting ceremonial song calming her.

More ebony bodies came towards her and surrounding her joining in with the singing, a sound that resonated deep within her, an echo of profound knowledge she had always known. A ceremonial song, for which ceremony she did not know but instinctively she began to run with them. And they ran for a long time until the song had finished.

The resting place was nothing to speak of, deep in the bush with a fire burning and around it some of the Aboriginals playing the digeridoo. Then they ceremonially carried the fire around her body to allow her to look at it for the last time. One of the tribesmen, a medicine man, led her into the bush. His music was haunting and she knew she must follow. As they went deeper into the bush night fell and he gestured her to lie on a bier of woven branches and be still whilst he sat at her head and proceeded to play his music and sing.

With only the light of the moon the velvety blackness of the night seemed to come to life. She saw a pair of bright eyes appear through the bush. She was in a deep mystical state and felt no fear. More eyes appeared until there were hundreds all coming towards her whilst the medicine man still played his music. Then the animals drew around her body and began to gently eat her body. She knew by the gentleness and care of their action that the animals in full awareness were aiding her entry back into mother earth. Some of the animals took a part of her to the medicine man. He offered it up to the moon and down to the earth and for the last time she saw her obsolete body taken back into nature.

Her body consumed, the medicine man instructed the animals to return to the bush. Their eyes drifted away from her sight, deep into the darkness, and the tune he played changed. She felt herself rise from the bier and shining in the moonlight she could see her new earth body. He told her that giving all her energies to the earth, nature would sustain her in her new consciousness and the animals would serve her. She was now firmly rooted back into the earth spirit and would be robed in a new natural body. She felt light and free of all the problems of her physical body and in union with all of life around her. She stayed until the song was finished and absorbing the last light of the moon she followed the medicine man back to the group.

The group welcomed her back amongst them, instructing her in the knowledge of earth magic. Showing her how to survive and live simultaneously within the earth and the physical world.

I have been back to the Aboriginal sacred land several times in vision. Over the many years, I have been taught several ceremonial healing practices and energy empowering techniques.

The Aboriginal ceremonies through vision demonstrated healing the split with our earth spirit within us. Bringing union in the psyche, preparing us for our eternal home. In my spiritual life in England I work with two aboriginal spirit guardians of the Dreamtime. They sing and play music in the psyches of the people who are to be gathered into the Dreamtime for eternal life and realise it before they leave their physical bodies. Some people feel more at ease working within other cultures, probably because their link to the earth spirit is stronger.

Entering the Dreamtime consciously can bring union with the spiritual and eternal opposite within the body. This spiritual reunion for most people happens only after physical death. If reached in life it can produce a profound passion in the body, unifying natural earth spirit energies of impersonal love. This is what is meant by going behind time to die into Love. Giving up all thought of self to nurture creation, not out of spiritual purity or to hide from the responsibility of Love, but to keep and sustain the flow of Love into Mother earth. For Love is not currently being honoured in the body sufficiently to sustain the earth.

Chapter xxxiii

The Sun Goddess

Her golden glow body stepped out of the sun
Proclaiming her new day on earth had begun.

Looking over the dry and arid wilderness of sand
She thought what beauty she could bring to this land,
Where man with God's blessing once reigned supreme
Broken down by thoughtless acts and now lay bare,
With no echo of God's voice his vibration anywhere.

Then God's retraction back into the sun
Scorched the land before the fires had begun,
To teach man his eternal lesson
Not to neglect the love of woman, the creation.

To purify this damaged earth
To which the Goddess in her Love gave birth,
God drew her tenderly back to Him
And in Love through the sun she left earth and man.

For in her return within, she could keep
Her creational beauty forever unique.

As she reached the sun centre
The serpent God made Love to her,
Uniting the points of power, becoming one
Bursting forth an eternal passion.

In this a new creation of beauty began,
She could bring once more onto earth,
Abundance of life, all green and plentiful.

Together with her consort at her side
God woman and the serpent, her guide,
Moving gently and gracefully out from the sun,
A new power for women here on the earth.

She waits for man's Love to stir again in his heart
That he too can herald in, with the Goddess,
The blessing of a bountiful new start

Until man awakens, the Goddess will stay
With her serpent God king all of the way.
Until the day dawning when he has the vision to see,
The spirit burning in her, in the depths of her being.

Then she in her Love and with the signal from God
Will give him back the serpent from the Garden was lost.

The Goddess with man as the Serpent-king,
Holding the kingdom in the eternal flame,
Burning bright, with the Love for all of creation.

The Golden Age

The Golden Age is not something to believe in or hope for as a future event. The Golden Age is now. I have worked extensively with people uniting them with the golden atom in their body, activating it so they can feel the power released inside come into being; their entry into the golden age.

I came to realise the true power and meaning of the union in Australia. Two weeks into the Barry Long course, I had absorbed much of my surroundings and the beauty of being with people of like minds. It was spring in Australia and getting hotter. The only respite from the heat was the occasional rainfall, bringing with it freshness to the camp that was most welcome.

After lunch I took a walk to the nearby freshwater lake and feeling comfortable in the cooling breeze I returned to the marquee for the next teaching session. Finding a seat at the front with a clear view of Barry, I sat down to listen. His theme today was about Love and partnership. I let nothing slip by, in total awareness of his voice vibration and its spiritual energy showing me in vision what he was saying.

His body began to glow with golden light emanating from his solar plexus, which radiated out to engulf him. She saw his body unfold and open to reveal inside all of life; the Garden of Love, life pristine and iridescent with the gentle trickle of a stream and a profound stillness. And in the golden radiance was revealed a golden body looking out at the people from inside of him. It stepped out of his physical body and walked down the steps towards her.

She sat in amazement, but there was no reaction from the people around her; no one else could see. As the golden man walked nearer she could feel a soft yielding in her body and the vibration of spiritual energy, a soft pressure in need of release. Then her golden body stepped out and he gathered it to him and returned back up the steps. Barry's body opened out to receive both golden forms inside, into the Garden of Love. An incredible feeling of profound Love and oneness overwhelmed her body. A vibration of boundless life energy, a deep feeling of joy and sweetness bringing with it a smile to her lips, a glow in her eyes and a deep sense of union and homecoming in her heart.

I had a chance to speak to Barry after the session and we talked together about my visions of our two golden bodies. In acknowledgement of the Love I had embodied he gave me the name Bhagavathi, saying he had only encountered the embodiment of eternal Love in woman once before in his lifetime. I sat silently until the approach of a friend brought me back to my senses.

It is my delight to be with eternal Love and know that Love in pure spirit form. I have been shown how to receive the Love and how to release it. Being behind time in the sacred land with the energy of Love, I can see golden bodies interacting with nature and with people I work with. I see their golden bodies yielding and unifying with the golden glow. It is my pleasure, with the love of the spirit, to help the people who need assistance and initiation into the Golden Age.

Each day when I wake I see the earth as the Paradise God intended it to be. There are no cycles of death and decay. It is of no matter to me when I die in my body because I have overcome suffering and time. When I die back into nature I will be immediately in Paradise with my opposite, my eternal golden man.

Chapter xxxiv

The Fig

I took life's walk and then I found a silver fig on the ground.
Shining bright it caught my eye; I knew not what in it did lie.
Beckoning to me to take a bite, I did, and I transformed that
*   night.*
With morning dew, I looked again, before my eyes two sides fell
*   apart,*
And then I heard a whisper; "I kept you perfect in my heart".

The silver fig changed to gold and as I looked my heart was
*   told.*
For I saw the golden male take gently the female from behind
*   the veil.*
With Love complete once more on earth, there will be no more
*   time for hurt.*
A new door awaiting to be opened, for loneliness has gone
*   forever,*
Joined in spiritual Love once more see the golden key turn in
*   the door.*

For heavens bliss here on this earth, a gift from our creator's
*   source.*
Mother earth whispers "I have more", the wind she follows
*   with a roar,*
"Do not use this Love self-serving, for I will banish you forever.
I give your heart another day, with this gift I show you the
*   way.*
Leave it in my care and keeping, my heart is big I know no
transgression.

Children of the earth you see, I have planted another tree
Full of fruit, almost ripe, ready for harvest, dearest to me.
This time I will catch them all, I will not allow them on foul
  ground to fall,
Until my children have all been found.

Their new spiritual Love is with earth's new creation,
Singing the song of the cycle of perfection,
Moving in what stays as new, it is Love that brings it all to
  you.
Divine Love that never grows old never weakens, never cold.

With Love's strongest hold I offer to you a vision,
A mystical pathway that was told in times gone by, but not lost
  forever,
I bring this story to your mind, your new sacred path back
  together.
I closed the fig, kept it locked, I alone know its secret untold,
Then when lovers they do meet, I allow them to keep this
  perfection in me.

With their Love locked firmly in my heart, I give you a clue of
  where to start.
I, the Mother wait for you all, are you going to ignore me till I
  call?
My cry and call is your earth disasters; follow the new road I
  have unfolded.
Walk with me into the sacred garden and there you will see,
One golden fig for each couple on my tree.

You can only enter as lovers; Love will carry you over time and
  space,
With grace and into your loving creators' arms.
I the Mother of this earth offer you this eternal birth.
The truth can never be misused, for you have to live it here and
  now.

Take the road Love lays for you, your golden fig is shining new,
One for each and every couple. I breathe the breath of new life
  into you.

Chapter xxxv

Sacred Knowledge

The Revealer came into my vision, as he stood there in his radiance I felt anticipation in me and I knew something enthralling was about to happen. He captivated my inner vision showing me that the inner spiritual and outer physical worlds had retained there balanced. Now he said it was time for me to interface all the worlds I had worked in. For spiritual energy cannot be activated sufficiently without this equilibrium.

I had no idea what it all meant in terms of being a workable area in life, but the Revealer assured me there was great purpose in why I had survived. His purpose was not only to help me hold the love but also to take me into the mind of the past, beyond the valley of the shadow of death, directing and showing me the significance of making the death energy fully conscious.

In my physical life I had experienced death whilst in hospital due to the embodiment of the Love energy that weakened my physical body. This energy works in the creation to promote the earth renewal. In its impersonal nature, life ensures the energies have no involvement in whether the body lives or dies. The energies had served their purpose but I still survived.

The Revealer told me that I must go beyond death consciously and that my mind has to know what purpose death holds. My mind had already gone through a transformation and its affect on me was stunning. Following the spiritual law of the opposites in my body this was to manifest in my life, fusing the two worlds together for my self and those I worked with.

The Revealer told her to have no fear for what He was about to reveal would take her through death back to life and join her to the mystery of creation. He took her to an ancient land where they walked to a distant burial chamber closed off with boulders long ago. He knelt to place a blue flame before the stones and directed her to watch the scene in front of her unfold.

As she walked through the time barrier he had opened with the blue flame, She heard the hoot of an owl as it flew up the open passageway and into the stone chamber where the Revealer sat. Buried beneath the earth mound the chamber was dark, but by the flame emanating from Him she knew there were others there. A wise woman was seated on a rock, at the entrance. The Death Goddess, elected to carry and connect the dying to the place in nature where the never ending cycle of life is continued; the sacred rite of passage through death back to life, to link with God and the divine Womb in woman to creation.

The Death Goddess stood as the village women brought their dying to the chamber. They laid them on the earth and tended to them, covering their naked bodies with herbs and oils. Silent and ever watchful, the Death Goddess remained alert keeping vigil over the dying, Her purpose connecting her to them at all times. Her compassion and Love for the continuation of the cycle of life provided the energy to hold and keep them conscious through the valley of death. The life essence within the wombs of their bodies was gathered up into a single flame and returned to the cycle of life; back to nature for regeneration.

She could see the women working among the dying, murmuring reassurance and easing them with a herbal liquid.

They cradled and rocked the dying as they sang haunting
songs of the earth, with beautiful words to carry the dying
effortlessly into death on the echo of their voices, for the dying
need to be kept partially conscious to keep the cycle of life alive.
The gentle tones of their singing drifted around the chamber
evaporating any negative past energy hanging in the air.
Ensuring this consciousness that is connected to the woman's
womb, its purpose is to imbibe their minds with their new
spiritual and sacred home, relieving suffering in the
transmission. The Death Goddess stood firm in Her resolve to
keep the dying conscious with Her Love and compassion and
the words of the songs of death.

The ceremony of death used to be one of the most sacred and
natural rites. The job of the Death Goddess and Her
attendants is to lead the dying through the passage of death,
through the Womb to link back into nature ensuring the
continuation of eternal love and life. This is the power of the
rite of passage. For at the beginning of time woman did not
have an ego consciousness only an earth spirit. This amazing
consciousness can be realised before physical death, if we can
allow the ego to die before the body. The body can be keep
alive by the earth energy, maintaining the earth's conscious
creation to continue. This is the freedom woman craves, to
unveil the mystery of the beauty of the earth visible all
around. The cry of the Death Goddess can still be heard today
in the body psyche of those She calls.

One Step Ahead Of The Death Energy
Outside the chamber there was a commotion of shouting and
fighting as the women tried to stop a group of men from
entering. Mindless of the purpose of the sacred ritual,
weapons grimly in hand, they brutally robbed the dying of
their few keepsakes and treasures carried with them to link the
two worlds of inner spiritual and outer physical; offerings for
the earth Mother and sky God.

The owl hooted once more and in the moonlight she saw the anguish on the women's faces as they tried to comfort the dying moaning in distress, in a desperate attempt to keep the life to-death-to life cycle alive within their bodies. But the sanctity of the chamber had been desecrated and the work to make the dying conscious destroyed. The sacred vigil could no longer continue and at daybreak the women rolled massive boulders across the entrance to the tomb, blocking it forever, closed off in anger against the blindness of man's brutality.

She found herself back outside the tomb before the stones with the blue flame burning. Then the flame blazed even stronger and the boulders rolled slowly back. The Revealer beckoned her towards Him and took her hand and they walked forward into the tomb. Inside there were several small chambers and in one He laid her on the ground and placed himself at her head.

In the chamber sealed off until now from the outside world in stillness and silence, the Revealer maintained the sacred vigil over her to connect her to her inner spiritual realms. As she lay there on the earth, with the moonlight shining through the chamber entrance, she felt deeply at peace.

Then she heard the compassionate cry of the Death Goddess calling to her, telling her that She would watch over her with the animals of the night whilst her body went through death and its energy was gathered into the divine flame and purified. With the essence of everyone who has ever achieved death consciously in that chamber, her body was supported through death and regenerated back to life bringing with it the Love and hidden sacred knowledge drawn from the earth, to be revealed to her in the fullness of time.

The Revealer kept her alert so she could connect with this ancient truth and resurrect the cycle of continuance in her own body and thus linking eternally with life and Love. He explained that it is conscious love that keeps the planet flourishing and the people conscious in death. If too many people died unconsciously the cycle of life would be broken. The human race would die out and the divine Womb and earth Paradise would be no more.

As He watched over her she felt the pure compassion of the Death Goddess enter her body. The feeling at times was overpowering, but it led her consciously back into the Womb of life and she knew, at the moment of descent into death, the purpose and her part in the cycle of life. The Revealer had taken her through the valley of life eliminating the valley of the shadow of death. She was united with the truth of her creativity through her life-giving Womb, the divine Womb of creation and with the serpent, the pure principle of man and his Love for woman.

She was taken through the life-death-life cycle many times to ignite the divine flames in her Womb. For it was her life purpose to bring back to the physical world the lost ceremony of death and to ignite in other women the divine Womb of life to continue the cycle of creation. To gather and contain within her physical body the earth and cosmic energies and channel them into the physical world to keep the life to-death to-life cycle in life flourishing.

Staying one step ahead of the death energy at all times by keeping a conscious connection to all life through the earth womb, will defeat death's sting. Eventually when the body falls away the wearer will not suffer but be at peace, united with the Paradise earth. The Revealer led me to the final death of the body, to make the death energy fully conscious in me. Changing my ego awareness to an earth spirit consciousness, my freedom in time. This has to be realised on all levels if possible. With the earth energy in the form of flames ignited in my Womb by the Love of the Revealer, I was reconnected to eternal life through death. I had found the truth behind the replica body, all my fear of death had been vanquished and many spiritual truths made known to me.

To ignite the flames of woman's spiritual Love, her link with God and her true nature of Love, woman must enter and die into her own Womb consciously. This can be done with man if he truly loves her, but if man chooses not to fulfil his purpose, as is increasingly happening now; she must resurrect it within herself as I have done.

My endeavour is to reinstate our link to the eternal cycle, the Paradise earth created through the Womb and Tomb of woman and to bring out the true nature and purpose of woman and man. To herald in this Golden Age I call for the honouring of woman, the creator of the earth through her creative Womb with man of Love at her side.

Chapter xxxvi

The Earth Barrow

Several years after I entered the earth barrow and went through the life-death-life cycle within my body, the Revealer directed me to take those working closely with me, who had joined with me in Love, to an ancient sacred site deep in the earth on our land.

It was late autumn and the weather was changeable when we reached the massive guard stones of the long barrow that night. One moment there was bright moonlight, the next heavy rain. We were glad to enter into the stone chamber beneath the earth mound where we settled ourselves and were warm and reasonably comfortable. Lighting our candles we gave homage to the earth, each person giving their own special thanks.

The Revealer said he would show me the reason for the breakdown and misuse of the ancient barrows and what they once represented. As the women listened in the bosom of the earth, the Revealer took me into vision and I was back in the ancient lands.

Across the field she could see a settlement of turf huts. In the twilight were hundreds of unkempt people gathered as if preparing for a ceremony. A group of the village men had lit a large bonfire. The women and children began to run and hide in their huts and the surrounding woodland. As the fire raged the men went around searching and she could hear screaming and shouting as they dragged out the sick, both young and old. The women began to wail in horror as all the deformed and maimed the dead and the dying, people and animals were thrown into the flames.

With the passage of time the women became conscious enough to know that this behaviour was inhuman and must not continue. Together they went to see the wise woman of the village, a visionary despised by some. She looked into her clear pool of water to see what they should do. They saw a chamber in the earth and were shown how to build it for the dying people, the sacred ceremonies they needed to perform to prepare them for death. This would enable them to stay conscious as they passed from this life to the next, thus keeping the life-death-life cycle alive in nature. For dying in fear prevents this cycle.

Through the vision I understood that even in early times woman, her ego awareness not yet fully formed, was in contact with the inner world, her earth spiritual nature. It isn't the dark arts people are afraid of, it's the fact that man used his superior strength and intellect to shut down her connection to the earth spirit within, hypnotising her into an intellectual loveless world. Creating fear in both woman and man, by denying the truth of our origins. Somewhere locked up in him from the far distant past he is terrified she will find out the truth of man and desert him.

Being denied this truth is not only a violation of the sacred rites of life and death but also the destruction of the Womb of the earth, the Womb of woman. In our modern world this has become common practice. It is up to the people who are prepared to save this earth to realise this and to stop its loveless desecration. But nothing can be destroyed in the spirit and earth woman today can enter the sacred Womb of the spirit where God can and will love out of her the suffering programmed in. This will bring her mind back to the beauty it once was, so she knows her connection to the earth Womb and her true spirit at all times.

The cycle of creation has been maintained until recent times through ancient rituals, such as the American Indian Happy Hunting Ground and the Aboriginal Dreamtime. But increasingly, with time, man has forgotten the mystery of creation through the divine Womb that is woman. Projected onto Paradise earth he has chosen to build his own fragmented world of suffering, confusion and loneliness through the ego awareness.

Rebirth and resurrection of the beauty of life through the creative Womb is only possible when man and woman are humble and honest enough to honour it, as some are endeavouring to do. This will bring them back to the truth, stopping the senseless thinking that God is only the male principle and not the female principal. Nothing can come into life without the Womb of woman, and the earth. Yet man chose to be banished from the garden of Paradise with the woman he made, to create his own world on this earth ruled by the mind, the oppressor of the female principle of pure Love. It is the mind that perpetuates this world of lovelessness and requires man and woman to Love the replica body's image before the spiritual essence within, the beauty of the creative Womb. Their sacred and spiritual place where the true Love between man and woman resides.

The Serpent

The Revealer explained to me that the time was now right to redress and realign our balance to the earth womb, so we were instructed to prepare our bodies for the creative energies. I wondered what was coming next, as I relayed what I had learnt to the women with me in the earth barrow. We felt privileged to be there and to take part in the resurrection of the sacred knowledge and settled down for the night in anticipation that more was to follow.

There was torrential rain outside now and she could not sleep. During the night the Revealer standing in the blue pillar of fire stepped out from her body. Then she saw the great serpent encircling the earth .It moved towards the barrow and thrust its way through the opening to weave up through the body of each woman in turn, up through the top of the head. The serpent repeatedly circled down to the centre of the earth and back up to the barrow to the women to collect the vital energy and instil it in their wombs. A compacted energy to ignite the new spiritual Womb connected to the earth through which the creator can love them.

The Revealer broke in again and I could see the flame of His eternal essence move around everyone and we all began to stir, feeling the Love and the power begin to enter our bodies. Then I saw the Revealer standing at the head of the chamber with the Death Goddess by His side. She called me to perform the ancient death ceremony that I had undergone several years earlier to prepare the women for the new earth spiritual awakening of their true nature. This changed their ego awareness to the new earth spirit of love of all life in the creation.

I rose and with the early morning sun peeping over the horizon I began to sing the song of the Goddess, of Her beauty and the grace of Her power to resurrect the Womb within woman which creates all of life on this earth. The women sang with me and the vibration of their voices rose all around and there was sweetness in the air, which we had never experienced before. It entered our bodies and we felt the profound stillness you feel when you know you have connected to the spiritual flame of divine Love, the presence of God.

The Goddess energy was all around them in the sweetness and the presence and the devotion they felt was overwhelming. Then the Death Goddess sang each woman through the tunnel of life to death and back to life again. There was an inrush of energy as She entered each woman in turn, igniting a flame in her Womb, the flame of the compacted energy of conscious death united with all life. And the Revealer held the compacted energy in timeless union as the serpent thrust forward encircling them together as one body; one Womb to ignite a second flame of compacted energy to fertilise the seeds of creation to carry into the New World.

The Revealer came to me and explained He needed small groups of women connected to the earth, who had gone through the life-death-life cycle to keep the fertilisation of the planet alive. Without the impersonal Love of creation there is no fertilisation, no planet of Love, no Paradise for couples of Love to enter into the Golden Age. This is a testament to those women who were there with me present in Love in the earth Womb and who felt at one with Mother earth.

They sat with her in the stillness and silence until the early morning sun came up to greet them and the most glorious sight made itself known to her. All of life in the form of pure pristine nature poured forth from the women around her in the barrow. It flowed out from between the two flames ignited in their Wombs and back into nature, into the countryside around them for the new creation.

The fertilisation had taken place and without the presence of man. The Revealer and the female principle, in the form of the Death Goddess and the serpent, which circles the cosmos, accomplished all. The women felt the profundity of what had taken place and the experience began a new cycle of change in their lives. Woman would not have to take this responsibility if love was free of corruption. This is a tragic tale of how love has been abused in this world.

By connecting all life force energy into our own Wombs, back into the whole, we have taken the responsibility for both male and female Love to secure the survival of the planet, to perpetuate the fertility; the creational energy of the earth. By connecting all life force energy into our own Wombs the continuation of all life is ensured. Woman, her Womb and the earth are one as they always have been, connected by man of Love for eternity.

Chapter xxxvii

The Goddess Witch

The hatred of the seer, which still continues today through the fear of the mystic mind, led earth woman to conceal her spiritual nature with a cloak and hide her earth knowledge in the form of spells to keep them safe.

The witches brew, rich and sweet,
From the cauldron strong and neat,
With many cats gathered at my feet,
I weave the web of spells.

When man degraded woman,
Blessed of God, he failed to see and hold his Love.
He called her Witch but man distorted Love
Never to know the truth.

The Witch repulsed him with crooked nose and warts,
Her protection to keep love pure.

With no man projecting onto her,
She gathered her spells, hidden in a log,
Put on her cloak, her disguise,
No man saw the Goddess behind the eyes.

With spell in heart, her secret law,
She moved throughout the spheres with ease,
To call all Goddess's to the crossing
To give her access across the void into time
The great hall bordering time, she knew well.

Manifesting her Goddess gown,
The Witch and the Goddess united as one
Went out into the crowds to see what hell had begun.

Man thought he had time all sewn up,
He forgot he had taught her mistrust.
She mastered it and kept her law,
Behind the cloak, she knew all.

She then showed him his illusion,
In failing in Love, he used it for his own delusion,
He chose not to see the Goddess gown,
He forgot it was she who wore the crown.

Freedom from the imprisoned mind,
The Witch was forever liberated in time.
Keeping her eternal freedom,
She had the power to love all men.

From behind her cloak and her crown
Seeing the truth of Love in creation,
Man, failing to see through his illusion
Distorting Love from the inside out,
The world, the mirror, the truth of it all.

She holds the power, there is no collusion,
Safe the spell that opens her mystery door,
Which man can only master when he is free of the world.
The Witch Goddess keeps Love forever pure
Safe in the knowledge, the spell held all.

The Many Faces of Man

Earthman struggles forward, unaware of his disguise,
He does not want the trouble or the lies.
But expedience and money now is his law,
Compelled to sacrifice his Love to serve the world.

Rolling aimlessly forward towards destruction
He can see no solution.
Shrugging his shoulders in hopeless despair
He has been made powerless because he cares.

From where did all this madness come
The killing and suffering: he wants it gone.
He must change direction with vision strong,
God man inside him calls to bring all life back as one.

To practice peace, this is earthman's right
God man inside will guide him; the time is now right.
Echoes from an earthly lesson learned long ago:
The pain endured from leaving his passion, woman the earth.

Earthman within is truly pure wisdom,
Rising from the depth of his being
To heal and balance all life, our troubled world scene.
Keeping control of his alien mind, his forceful will
Solves the problem, but will he hear?

Rocketing forward recklessly, out of control
Is all alien man on earth can know.
Ready to kill offspring, lover and friend
Until God man calls from inside, then his time is at an end.

In his mind alien man is destined to fill the time he has
  written,
To desecrate the earth, woman's glory to the end.
Trying to usurp God by violence and force
Manifesting more karma, paying service to his will,

Before realising his destructive crime kills.
Never to reach God of Love in this way;
Leaving more debts for humanity to pay,
Escaping our earth to live on dead planets

Not claiming his works, the world he has made,
Cloaking his kingdom, leaving behind
Desolation, confusion and pain.
In the end, what does alien man gain?
A loveless planet for his mental games.

God man intervenes to relieve earth of Her pain,
Knowledge man knows from his far distant past.
Resurrecting this truth will restore balance again
And His right, to His claim

This is earthman's integrity, until he has the power to see
His alien mind of destruction serves nothing but grief and
   pain.
Many earthmen will acknowledge the God impulse from
   within,
To right the earth's planet made in Love by him

Medicine fails us, science too,
But God man of wisdom will see us through.
Earthman realised with the authority to see
That the earth Womb of woman gives to all freely.

Never denies the world its abundance and wealth
To feed her children, flowers of the earth.
Is this how humanity serves her grace?
The mother of all does not need our heartless neglect.

Time to change course, the lesson now learnt:
Woman with God, with discernment and power to change,
Will wipe out and finish alien man's earthly games
Sacrificing alien man to save the creation.

Retracting the life force back into her Womb
To build a New World of Love, denying alien man
Evan in her earth Love and power of giving,
Alien man has stayed indifferent, violent and blind.

Moving towards God in the depth of her being
She has tried all in loving and giving,
To where only earthman of Love can enter in,
The Goddess in her wisdom knows no other solution.

Until the day dawns and man has the power to see,
Earth woman is God too,
Treat her tenderly.

Chapter xxxviii

The Spiral

In the spiral of all vital life, with the energy we call Love pivoted at its centre taking form in matter, all life comes together gracefully laid upon our earth. This great intelligence of the movement of God is the means to give and receive of the omnipotent presence. Rising out of the stillness in the centre, is the blue flame of pure Love, the vapour of divine inspiration, God's will.

It is God's law, passion and pleasure to give all people and all life on this earth, no matter what shape, colour, or creed, this droplet of Love which in time will carry them back to the Creator, back to the great eternal fire of all life. Free of the mind's involvement or interference, God dwells in this form of Love in the people and all have a chance to unify and fulfil this omnipotent power.

People are cut off from spiritual Love through the interference of the mind and are suffering from lack of this Love. Throughout the ages there has been more than sufficient demonstration of the cruelty of the mind and that the supremacy of Love is the only thing that can set us free. Every one of us carries the eternal essence the spark of God's inspiration, the blue flame, our entry into the sacred lands.

The first rule of Love is we must stop thinking that someone else carries the key to our salvation. . In the first instance, the only thing that opens the door to Paradise is our own Love we make with each other, making God consciousness, then drawing God nearer to you. The mind is the only barrier to

Love. We each have the power to overcome this while on the earth. We must endeavour to prevent the alien outsider, the interfering mind that has not yet reached Love, from trying to enter the sacred space, the point of perfection within.

Man in the Garden of Love violated spiritual law with his first thought, thinking he knew better than God. He thought he could love woman more than God. In taking partial jurisdiction over Love and woman, man brought death with the replica body into being. God in his wisdom allowed man his freedom so he could realise in time the mistake he had made

God gave man the power to find woman in the Garden, this precious formless Love made from creation and the nectar of God. Man desired to take this Love to create the earth and the thinking world. Pure woman was too sacred to bring into man's world so man made replica bodies, then taught her how to love sexually.

In our earthly spiritual body in the Garden before time, we chose with God's will to, take on the task of correcting the malfunction of the suffering mind that knows no Love. . We sacrificed ourselves for this purpose it is the reason for all the suffering the human race has endured, for what seems forever and its getting worse.

We were ejected from the core of the earth to a new dimension of existence on the surface of the earth, on the periphery of our true consciousness, reflections in time. That is when human love through the replica body came into being. In denying us the fire of our earth spirit passion, we were taught how to love through pleasure. This teaching oppressed the pure female principle and we lost the power to be in the Creators presence in the divine triangle, man, woman, with God consciousness, renewing the paradise we lived in.

Our purpose in life's walk is to purify the mind so that the divine spark of pure Love can enter, carrying with it insights of our sacred and spiritual home, relinquishing past torment. Only then will the two worlds be in balance and we will be free. Human love purified of all suffering.

With their new physical bodies prepared, God infused a portion of the pure essence from the sacred garden, contained in the sacred space within, for them to Love and connect with The Creator. God kept the greater portion of the Love in reserve, the nectar, the pure flesh of man and woman with which to draw man and woman back through the blue flame with their Love. Opening the doorway back to the sacred eternal place of divine Love.

We are still in shock from the first moment thought entered us in the Garden, the shock of putting into action this life of suffering that cannot be stopped. Humans love a dream in time. We didn't succeed in purifying the mind through human love, now it is up to every individual to consciously travel the path home to build their paradise with their eternal opposite within.

Only the command of God when we turn back to Divine Love will stop the cruelty, to bring us back to our earthly senses. For there is no mastery over Love on this earth, for there is no person, man or woman, at peace on this earth and freed of sexual imprisonment. Divine Love can never be mastered only consciously died into. Love comes to master you and will do all to capture you in its embrace. The mastery is if you can live it. Dying into Divine Love is our natural state and divine right here on Earth. To be connected to the Creator at all times no matter what situation you find yourself in, finally transporting you back to life, the whole, with dignity and grace. God, the two principles of life is there for all that have had enough of the old system and ways of living in the past.

The blue flame will guide and protect you through all your spiritual development, if you put your confidence in it nourishing it with your love. Then the creator shows you in the flame, the never-ending glory of present truth, preparing you for your sacred and mystery journey home.

Human love is never enough for humanity it will never solve suffering on this planet, for human love always fail you. Can you stand Love? If you do not want it, or cannot take responsibility for it, it will leave you like a bird that has flown the nest, moving onto another body. This is the integrity of Divine Love, ensuring its uncorrupted and safe passage through time. If Love is not enough for you then you do not know Love.

And human Love will be free only when we cease trying to have wilful control over it, manipulating it for our personal involvement. With selfish conditional Love for others and the enslavement of the mind through religion and false teachings, robbing ourselves of Divine Love our true, pure, spiritual consciousness. Spiritual Love cannot be taught, it can only be lived. This is why we all must die, for then we are cleansed and purified of everything in human love that we chose to take on. To allow Love to master you, by dying into Love while alive and conscious, is vital to restore in you your true Godly nature and the full consciousness of your Divinity.

It is the most difficult thing to do on this earth, conscious physical death in life, but this can only be accomplished when man and woman have joined in life. Love will sustain you after conscious death and purification of the past. This purification enables you to keep the physical body and an active mind to go through the time barrier to another dimension of true consciousness, where you will never suffer again. Energetically, Love thus has the power with its grace to grant you a Paradise life on this earth, where man and woman can love freely without the distractions and distortion of this world. Holding the two worlds of corrupted human love and Divine Love in perfection and equilibrium. This is the mastery of Love.

Love is the only energy fine enough to keep the corruptible body clean after the life-death-life cycle has been completed here on this earth. The cycle cannot be done without the power of Love's cleansing, through the union of man and woman. Love can only stay with those who honour it. God will only let you enter the sacred space within the body when man and woman honour God through their Love for each other and restore the earth to its former beauty and glory. For lack of Love cuts us off from what sustains us.

The Golden bodies represent Love, the timeless union of our perfection in the Paradise earth where Love is always free. This is where you will find your true eternal beloved, Love's offering in truth, which over the aeons will never leave you.

The Golden Bodies

The two golden bodies were drawn together by the magnetic energy running through the golden cord that connects the beloved. The signal was strong. In an instant, they curled up into glowing golden balls of light and slipped down the cord toward their scintillating union. Glowing with Love for each other, unable to stand their separation a moment longer, the lovers touched. It was electric and the vibration went out through the earth, which responded with urgency, informing them it was time for union with Mother earth to sustain her continuation and bounty.

The magnetic power of Mother earth surrounded them and as they held each other in a firm embrace they allowed her mighty power to suck them down to a bubbling spring, sparkling invitingly; the entrance into the centre of the earth. With the sun energy of their union now absorbed in their golden bodies, they stepped in. Travelling at light speed through the onrushing waters, sparkles of reflected light like millions of stars lit their way, like a great kaleidoscope of colour bursting all around them.

They passed through the wondrous colours of the earth's crust watching the movement of life within. Down through the rich dark organic soil, down through the opaque silver-white chalk, to the russet brown and gold of dense rock formations. Following still the magnetic pull, they entered a labyrinth of dark tunnels and caves. There Mother earth stores the gases and fires of her passion in her bosom, awaiting the sun to penetrate the earth's inner core, to oscillate with its energy and then strike, to activate the inner core of the earth.

Undaunted by the urgency, the golden bodies continued on at light speed, carrying to her the compacted essence of the sun's golden radiance. Then suddenly they burst through, at the source of the underground spring, into a vast and silent underground cave where Mother earth beckoned forth in her stillness. They walked forward towards the supreme presence before them, the great pool of eternal life, and graciously and silently slipped in. Now joined with the eternal waters of all life, their golden bodies of Love began to glow and shimmer with the earth energies; Mother nature singing her song, a mighty vibration in acknowledgement of their Love bringing the earth and the cosmos together in union. And the cave was lit up with an invincible radiance. Mother Earth's energy burst forth from the cave igniting the gasses with her fiery passion, erupting out through the earth's molten core into the creation. And the fiery heat surrounded every seed in the earth Womb and on the earth's surface, and each seed yielded to her passion, opening with a crack and the husk fell away, bearing the life force to nourish the planet.

The continuance of the creation through woman's Womb, for the existence of the earth with her beloved, thus was assured.

208

And through this still and silent pool, eternal life and conscious Love are accessible whilst still in the physical body here on this earth, an eternal blessing.

The Vortex and the Centre of Stillness

The vortex and the still centre is the action to move couples together in Divine Love and is poised, ready in the sensory world around us that we know as creation. But without acknowledgement of Love for each other, the power to bring Love into our world is denied. Unless able to enter the physical body through Love, all forms of energy enter nature to create havoc to wake us up. God, gracefully and patiently with gentle movement through creation, waits forever still in the mists behind time. Balanced between the two worlds, God's presence in the form of the flame will release from our world and unite in the golden radiance those who are ready and cannot reach it through human love. Nobody can stop or deny or destroy life and the great spiral of life makes sure that spark of God's consciousness comes to live, and live again.

The Mists

The mists rose high over the mountain stream,
God's consciousness gathers in the unseen.
Deep within that movement, my knowing saw,
Forming behind time, a flame, a droplet pure.

One thought, an inspiration, a movement from God;
God's will, the truth rushing forward into our world.
One spark of life, a God given ideal,
The will to live, the struggle, the fight
One breath of life ready poised on the edge of time;
To live again, to live always,
This message the eternal spark will bring.

Life that fades and ebbs away,
Comes to live through the spark another day.
This day of renewal, the whole of our being,
Cannot be extinguished in one creation.
This mammoth wave, the unseen power,
God's being in the movement towards that hour.

The earth renews itself through Love,
Its children the stars, in alignment with Love.
The sun, the moon, in timeless rhythm
Enchanted earth's children from the beginning.
God's will intact in the children of earth.
For in their knowledge they will give birth
To a new law spoken but not yet lived.
Encoded in our hearts we feel
Our new destination we know made real
.

Deep within from the unknown eternal fountain of truth,
These laws will rush forward into our mind,
Renewing the people, God's own kind.

Epilogue

Many years have gone by since my spirit double fled through the circle of fire into the inner spiritual realms to join with the Revealer and the Goddess, and I wondered what would herald in her return. I was deeply embedded with them there on the inside but I had not yet been able to return with my twin through the circle of fire back into the outside world. I had no idea if a permanent return to the physical world would sever my link with the Revealer and the Goddess and my spiritual life. My Love for humankind and my family had always been an inspiration to me and I wanted to fully live this life I had been born into. My call was answered.

The Goddess, in her naked golden body, rose from the depths of the spirit realms up to the molten heart of the golden sun, to meld with the sun centre in glorious union. Her union complete, She left the sun to walk the shores of the inner spiritual realms to unite with the waters of life. Walking through the waves She entered deep into the lagoon, gracefully connecting with all marine life. Swimming with dolphins and shoals of fish weaving all around her. She rose up to the sacred eternal pool, connecting the worlds into which all life flows, to join with the Revealer by the blue pillar; the union of the pure principle of woman and man in the presence of God.

She cloaked herself in an iridescent gown of light to prepare herself for the union, and I saw in Her body the seeds of all life, some She carried in a small basket of light. She walked forwards in Her serenity to pass through the blue pillar, in need of recognition and permission from the divine, for the union to take place. The Revealer stood silently waiting on the other side, honoured to be granted this union by God in this pool of all life. The sacred Womb and Tomb containing the flames of creational energy in His safe keeping awaiting Her presence. The earth Womb He has prepared with God in His need of the pure principle of woman, to bring the creational energy into being.

He walked towards Her as She emerged from the pillar and they joined together in joyful elation. She sprinkled the seeds from her basket of light into each of the flames in His care. As the flames fertilised the seeds they burst into a profusion of colour, the whole of the created world, flowers, trees, animals and birds on the inside and outside of life.

Seeing that their union was perfection and approved by God, I was now happy inside to know all was in balance in the earth Womb. Many weeks went by and occasionally I could see the Revealer with the Goddess and I wondered at how close to the physical world She could now come.

My daughter was to be married, the wedding was a grand affair and made a strong impression on my mind. The bride and groom and family and friends dressed in their finery and the beauty of the ceremony honouring the Love of my daughter and her man for each other was so much like the beauty of my inner visions, a great movement of energy began within me.

Two days after the guests had gone, I sat down to rest and my awareness was brought back abruptly to the inner realms. The Revealer stood silently waiting. I saw light emanating from him and in a split second I saw the whole of my journey through other worlds come together. The American Indian Happy Hunting Ground, the Aboriginal Dreamtime, all my various life forms including my last and final body now being prepared.

Standing in a circle, the mystic Goddesses sang her out of a living tree laid out on the ground as the cross had been.

212

Calling on the moon, they chanted their spells and as the chanting intensified the power and light of the moon cracked open the tree to enter her body and instilling within her, her new earth spirit re-awakened back into time. As the mystic Goddesses sang in unison, she rose and walked among them guided to wait and be still a while.

Then the light of the moon moved down from the starry sky to lift her body and she rose above them, to start the long journey back through the underworld. She moved into the marshlands of the underworld, propelled at great speed, enfolded by the lunar intelligence drawn forever upwards through the darkness. Then she saw above her the great fiery light of the burning black cross with the circle of flames she had come through many years before.

She hesitated for a moment, uncertain, but the power of the moon still strong within her assured her all was well. She floated with ease towards it, up to the centre and passed through the circle, back into the dark field, back into her mind and into life. Then from on high in the sky turning back to look below, she saw the cross had crumbled into smouldering ashes, with one single flame burning where the centre had been.

The purification and union through the flames was complete, and my cycle of time on the cross now closed.

The Revealer spoke, saying that no purity can come into existence without first healing and purifying all wounds of the past. The tiny flame at the centre of the cross is the crossover point in our minds allowing the divine essence to enter in. For woman this is the Goddess and for man, God, filling their minds with creation and life's purpose.

My earthly life had been purified enabling me to unite my spirit twin with the wisdom of the Goddess from all the spiritual realms and to bring them both back to their rightful place in my life. The Revealer, the pure principle and wisdom of man, moves with the serpent and the Goddess in the earth Womb of creation within my physical body, keeping me in touch with God through the passion. It is this passionate enlightenment that I intend to give to all the people I meet who are ready to receive it.

The Lovers

Holding hands, walking the shores of time
The Lovers faced each other
Fathomless depths transmitting
Timelessly between each others eyes

Enfolded by a caressing breeze
God called, they entered the ebb and flow
Dancing the rhythms of the divine

The gold of the sun hung like a jewel in the sky
The moon drawing them ever nearer
God beckoned, they slipped silently behind the veil of this
  world
Entering the sacred land

The Sun and Moon Union

They could see the sun and the moon are linked together in timeless interaction: the sun, the spirit of cosmic man and the moon, the spirit of the earth Goddess who watches over her creation, giving her energy to the earth for all nature and life. The moon rose to greet the sun and as the sun gave its warmth and light to the moon it began to shine on the lapping waters of the shores of the dark pool behind time. Contained within, all life is there.

The moon moved down to the water to transform, offering her body of light to the earth and up to the sun, and the molten liquid surface became a silver mirror. In the magnificence of her power she spread herself across the earth and the dark waters of the sacred pool. Her all encompassing power too much to resist, unable to contain itself, the sun poured out its golden solar energy effortlessly, endlessly and still, into the silver sea.

A union of supreme effortless being, the two heavenly bodies danced in union in the giving and receiving of each other to bring all life into creation. Spiralling together down the matrix, down into their bodies in the figure of eight movement, the double helix of all life, bursting into colour and moving in their bodies to take them deeper into Love in the earth. They could see the energies dancing in the centre of her their bodies and they sensed the waves of lapping energy and a deep and profound feeling of joy, peace and Love unknown in this world. And they watched in wonderment at the brilliance of the Sun and Moon energy within them.

The Healing Book   by Chris Thomas & Diane Baker

This book is for those who wish to heal, starting at the beginning of the healing process with simple, easily followed exercises which can begin to unlock the healing potential which is inherent in all of us. Nobody needs to feel left out of these abilities. We are all healers, all that we need to do is to stop telling ourselves that we are not. Whatever level of experience you have of healing, this book explains in simple uncomplicated language that does not use mysticism or any form of ritual, how to understand the "Chakras" and the way in which our daily lives influence them, to relate medical conditions to the chakras and to learn methods which will bring the chakras back into balance, both for yourself and for others. These methods apply equally to humans and to animals. If you do not have any experience of giving healing, but would like to learn, this book can set you on that path. If you already work as a healer, in whatever capacity, and would like to explore your greater potential, this book is also for you. The authors have a combined experience of over twenty five years of providing healing and have taught very many people to unlock their own healing potential. This book is not only about learning to heal from the beginning, but also explores some of the energy manipulation techniques used by the authors in their daily practise as "Psychic Surgeons".   ISBN 186163 053 0   £8.95

Medicine for the Coming Age   by Dr Lisa Sand

Dr Lisa Sand, graduate of the Medical College of Pennsylvania has long been aware of the presence of post-traumatic stress disorder in all souls incarnated on planet Earth. It is the major cause of physical, emotional, mental and spiritual disorders and symptoms. Their variations are myriad and distressing, but relief is great when the cause can be eliminated. Fear, anger and frustration give way to joyous life fulfilment. In the last 23 years, Dr Sand has devoted herself completely to this task, together with selected mediums who have been her earthly collaborators, and a number of wonderful, highly skilled souls who are not now incarnate, but who have been very active indeed in participating in the work from the point of their unlimited vision and vast experience with human souls. This book is a joint statement and description of the work by all concerned through the pen of Dr Sand. Its purpose is to help heal and enlighten all who read it.   ISBN 186163 068 9   £9.95

The Fool's First Steps   by Chris Thomas

Are you asking Questions? Transforming? Wanting to know the purpose of it all? Do the old answers no longer work?   The true purposes of Avebury and Stonehenge and the knowledge contained there, stellar gateways, the origins of crop circles, changing Earth energies, the true nature of angels... Personal transformations happening now on a grand scale, mental, emotional and physical and realising the spiritual origins of the human race... If this book were a novel it would make fascinating reading, but as the explanations again and again strike a true chord, it makes compulsive and unforgettable reading which will help you change how you view life. ISBN 186163 072 7   £9.95

Self Enlightenment   by Mayan O'Brien

Are you on a quest for truth, knowledge and wisdom? If so, this book will be a guide and a stepping stone for you. *Self Enlightenment* is full of practical advice on many areas of life. It discusses meditation, visualisation, the aura, examining our lives, creating a mind map, using astrology, the University of the solar System (a guided visualisation), the Tree of Life, health and herbs and how to organise a retreat for yourself. This book can be seen as a beacon to illuminate your way. ISBN 186163 0484   £9.95

Vortex - The End of History   by Mary Russell

A book of transmissions through the mediumship of Mary Russell. Some of the souls who have given of their knowledge and observations from the world unseen were household names in one or more of their past sojourns in human bodies. Others come from worlds different to ours. Their collective aim is to inform us as much as possible of what is real and what is not, distinguishing between intellectual fantasy and true eternal science. In doing this, they point out where we came from and where we are going. Much of their message is to do with the great changes now occurring as well as greater ones to come as this planet heads towards a vortex in time. They are all designed to promote the progress of each human soul. The intelligence and the love in charge of it all, as glimpsed through these messages, is breathtaking and awesome in its grandeur. ISBN 186163 0832   £11.95

Working With The Merlin - Healing People and Planet by Geoff Hughes

The Merlin is a guardian of this planet, together with many others, and is acting on behalf of other unseen guardians, seeking mankind's help in restoring harmony to all here. This book is about the Merlin and his teachings in the 1980's and 1990's. He has awoken, for now is his time to move about the Land again to bring healing to the peoples, and the earth. The writer is, like many others, on a Quest for knowledge, to Know, to search for a meaning of life. The answers which came through are stunning, sometimes shocking, often controversial. This book is about aspects of this work, carefully graded to take the aspiring student through the first principles and onward into the realms of having the ability to make direct contact with the Forces of the Cosmos. Cutting through the mountains of superstition and man-made rules to find the simplicity and purity of our natural heritage of direct contact with the Unseen Worlds. ISBN 186163 0018   £10.95

Tarot Therapy vol 1 - Tarot for the New Millennium by Steve Hounsome

A groundbreaking new work proposing the use of the Tarot as a therapy, alongside the many other complementary and natural procedures available. This first of three volumes, 'Tarot for the New Millennium', explains the theory behind the idea of Tarot Therapy, tracing its origins and history in this light. The concept of both Major and Minor Arcanas are explored, showing the true, therapeutic construction of the pack. The book outlines methods of working with the Tarot as a therapy in consultations, adding many other ways in which it can be utilised in this manner. Volume 2 and 3 contain explorations of the Major and Minor Arcana cards in their therapeutic setting and use. This major new work on the Tarot represents a turning point in its evolution, which the author shows has always adapted itself to the needs of humanity since its inception Here is the method of working with the Tarot in the Aquarian Age, above and beyond its current position. ISBN 186163 074 3   £14.50

The Mystic Life of Animals   by Ann Walker

We are increasingly recognisng animals as spiritual beings worthy of our respect. "Communication is the golden key that unlocks the door to understanding." Animal communication is mostly concerned with emotions, feelings, events and happenings in the here and now. We tend to think that animal communication involves them understanding what we want, but in truth, it is a two-way process. A lifetime of living with and loving animals has led Ann Walker to conclude that much communication with animals is on a mind to mind level, and she tells of many personal psychic experiences with animals. Old superstitions and magical beliefs about animals are examined, also the attitude of different religions. Ann shares her own experiences and those of others with dead pets returning or sending messages and expresses a firm belief in the continued spiritual existence of animals after death.
ISBN 1861630166   £7.95

FREE DETAILED CATALOGUE

A detailed illustrated catalogue is available on request, SAE or International Postal Coupon appreciated. **Titles can be ordered direct from Capall Bann, post free in the UK** (cheque or PO with order) or from good bookshops and specialist outlets. Titles currently available include:

Auguries and Omens - The Magical Lore of Birds by Yvonne Aburrow
Caer Sidhe - Celtic Astrology and Astronomy by Michael Bayley
Call of the Horned Piper by Nigel Jackson
Celtic Lore & Druidic Ritual by Rhiannon Ryall
Earth Magic by Margaret McArthur
Enchanted Forest - The Magical Lore of Trees by Yvonne Aburrow
Familiars - Animal Powers of Britain by Anna Franklin
Healing Book (The) by Chris Thomas
Handbook For Pagan Healers by Liz Joan
Healing Homes by Jennifer Dent
Herbcraft - Shamanic & Ritual Use of Herbs by S. Lavender & A. Franklin
In Search of Herne the Hunter by Eric Fitch
Magical Guardians - Exploring the Spirit & Nature of Trees by P. Heselton
Magical Lore of Cats by Marion Davies
Medecine For the Coming Age, Dr Lisa Sand
Patchwork of Magic by Julia Day
Psychic Self Defence - Real Solutions by Jan Brodie
Sacred Animals by Gordon MacLellan
Sacred Geometry by Nigel Pennick
Sacred Lore of Horses The by Marion Davies
Secret Places of the Goddess by Philip Heselton
Talking to the Earth by Gordon Maclellan
Taming the Wolf - Full Moon Meditations by Steve Hounsome
Vortex - The End of History, by Mary Russell

Capall Bann is owned and run by people actively involved in many of the areas in which we publish. Our list is expanding rapidly so do contact us for details on the latest releases.

Capall Bann Publishing, Freshfields, Chieveley, Berks, RG20 8TF